T0328977

Cambridge Elements ≡

Elements in Musical Theatre
edited by
William A. Everett
University of Missouri-Kansas City

OFFENBACH PERFORMANCE IN BUDAPEST, 1920–1956

Orpheus on the Danube

Péter Bozó
*RCH Institute for Musicology/Liszt Academy of Music,
Budapest*

CAMBRIDGE
UNIVERSITY PRESS

CAMBRIDGE
UNIVERSITY PRESS

University Printing House, Cambridge CB2 8BS, United Kingdom

One Liberty Plaza, 20th Floor, New York, NY 10006, USA

477 Williamstown Road, Port Melbourne, VIC 3207, Australia

314–321, 3rd Floor, Plot 3, Splendor Forum, Jasola District Centre, New Delhi – 110025, India

103 Penang Road, #05–06/07, Visioncrest Commercial, Singapore 238467

Cambridge University Press is part of the University of Cambridge.

It furthers the University's mission by disseminating knowledge in the pursuit of education, learning, and research at the highest international levels of excellence.

www.cambridge.org
Information on this title: www.cambridge.org/9781108977593
DOI: 10.1017/9781108973410

© Péter Bozó 2022

First published 2022

A catalogue record for this publication is available from the British Library.

ISBN 978-1-108-97759-3 Paperback
ISSN 2631-6528 (online)
ISSN 2631-651X (print)

Offenbach Performance in Budapest, 1920–1956

Orpheus on the Danube

Elements in Musical Theatre

DOI: 10.1017/9781108973410
First published online: May 2022

Péter Bozó
RCH Institute for Musicology/Liszt Academy of Music, Budapest
Author for correspondence: Péter Bozó, pebozo@gmail.com

Abstract: As a legacy of the Habsburg Empire, performances of Jacques Offenbach's musical stage works played an important role in Budapest musico-theatrical life in the twentieth century. However, between the collapse of the Empire and the 1956 anti-Soviet revolution, political ideologies strongly influenced the character of these productions when they took place. Public performances of Offenbach's works were prohibited between 1938 and 1945 and they became the bases for propagandistic adaptations in the 1950s. This Element explores how the local operetta tradition and the vogue of operettas featuring composers as characters during the interwar period were also important factors in how Offenbach's stage works were performed in mid-twentieth-century Budapest, in versions that sometimes bore little resemblance to the originals.

Keywords: Offenbach, Budapest, political ideologies, performances, reception history

ISBNs: 9781108977593 (PB), 9781108973410 (OC)
ISSNs: 2631-6528 (online), 2631-651X (print)

Contents

1 Reconstructing the Legacy of Offenbach in Budapest

Probably the biggest cultural shock I have ever experienced was when I first watched a televised performance of Offenbach's *Orphée aux enfers* by the Lyons Opera Company, directed by Laurent Pelly. It happened somewhere around 2000, some years after the production was premiered at the Opéra de Lyon in 1997. Conducted by Marc Minkowski with Natalie Dessay in Eurydice's role, this superb performance was a revelatory experience. The real shock for me was not so much the quality of its presentation as just how good, and witty, the music itself was – and how strikingly the entire production contrasted with the staging of operetta as it is traditionally understood in Hungary. Fortunately, a DVD recording of the production was released, and the first thing I did during my Paris sojourn in 2003 was to purchase it.

The next surprise came in 2005 when the same piece was staged at a spoken theatre in Budapest. Hearing a work by Offenbach there at the beginning of the third millennium was quite a rare event. Not only was the staging completely different from the last performance I had attended but also, as a matter of fact, it was not even the same work, as neither the text nor the music resembled those of the Lyons production.

During the past fifteen years, I have tried to understand the reasons for this difference. The first step was to immerse myself in the secondary literature on the composer. Since there were no books or studies about him in my mother tongue, I studied the bibliographical survey published by three German authors in 1998.[1] Fortunately, it was possible for me to obtain the detailed and well-documented biography by Jean-Claude Yon, first published in 2000, which provided a fascinating overview not only of the composer but also of the historical and cultural context of his life and work.[2]

Yon's volume, together with Ralf-Olivier Schwarz's recent study,[3] reveals an unusual career. It narrates the story of a musician who, at the age of fourteen, settled in Paris in order to attend the Conservatoire and continue the violoncello studies he had begun in his native city, Cologne. However, he left the institution after about a year and became an orchestral musician, then a salon virtuoso. He finally became a theatrical composer, but not without a struggle. As a stage author, he made his debut in 1839, not with a full-length opera but as the co-author of musical interpolations in a vaudeville production. During the next decade and a half, he unsuccessfully tried to establish

---

[1] Christoph Dohr, Kerstin Rüllke, and Thomas Schipperges (eds.), *Bibliotheca Offenbachiana* (Cologne: Dohr, 1998); Beiträge zur Offenbach-Forschung, ed. Christoph Dohr, Vol. 1.

[2] Jean-Claude Yon, *Jacques Offenbach* (Paris: Gallimard, 2/2010 [1/2000]).

[3] See also Ralf-Olivier Schwarz, *Jacques Offenbach: Ein Europäisches Portrait* (Weimar: Böhlau Verlag, 2019).

himself in the Paris musical theatres as an opera composer. Until 1855, he had a lasting relationship with only one state institution, the Comédie-Française, which was, however, a spoken-word theatre. As the conductor of the French National Theatre (1850–5), his main task was to perform incidental music. However, in the year of the first Paris world exhibition, he founded his own theatrical enterprise, the Théâtre des Bouffes-Parisiens, which provided extremely popular musical stage works. At first, due to administrative restrictions, he created only short one-act pieces with just a few characters (*opérettes*). From 1858, beginning with *Orphée aux enfers*, he also began to create full-length evening works requiring bigger forces (*opéra bouffes*). During the next two-and-a-half decades, he proved to be an extremely successful stage composer, not only in Paris but throughout Europe. From 1857 on, his theatre company gave guest performances in London, Berlin, Brussels, and Vienna; his works were frequently played in such places as Munich, Hamburg, and Bad Ems. Around 1860, even the primary French theatres capitulated, although his *opéra-comique Barkouf*, premiered at the Opéra-Comique, and his ballet-pantomime *Le Papillon*, staged at the Opéra, had no lasting success. His reputation reached its peak in 1867, when his works were performed in no fewer than five theatres in the French capital. Following the 1870–1 Franco–Prussian War, the popularity of his pieces decreased somewhat. As the director of the Théâtre de la Gaîté, where he provided his spectacular *féeries* (fairy plays with lavish scenery and stage effects) like *Le Roi Carotte*, he went bankrupt, so that in 1876 he undertook an American tour in order to re-establish his financial position. At the end of his life, he was working on what is probably his best-known piece, the fantastic opera *Les Contes d'Hoffmann*. The first performance of this work, at the Opéra-Comique in 1881, was however already a posthumous premiere.

Since both the composer and his works intrigued me, after some time my research began to focus on the phenomena of Offenbach's reception in Budapest and its connection to the development of operetta there. The task was not easy as no systematic study of primary sources concerning his fortune in Hungary had been conducted before, although some sporadic performance data had appeared in such works as Loewenberg's *Annals of Opera*,[4] András Batta's popular monograph,[5] and Moritz Csáky's in-depth volume about the ideology of Viennese operetta.[6] This is all the more interesting since Western European

---

[4] Alfred Loewenberg, *Annals of Opera – 1597–1940* (London: John Calder, 1978).

[5] András Batta, *Träume sind Schäume: Die Operette in der Donaumonarchie*, trans. by Maria Eisenreich (Budapest: Corvina Kiadó, 1992).

[6] Moritz Csáky, *Ideologie der Operette und Wiener Moderne: Ein kulturhistorischer Essay zur österreichischen Identität* (Vienna: Böhlau, 1996).

research has produced important results over the past three decades concerning the composer's reception history: in 1999 a multi-authored volume was published documenting Offenbach performances in several European cities from London to Vienna; its editor, Rainer Franke, urged the investigation of the composer's Eastern European reception.[7] A shorter study of a similar subject in French was published in 2003 by Yon himself, whose witty title can be translated into English as: 'The Posthumous Career of a Musician, or Offenbach in the Underworld'.[8] It is also worth mentioning Laurence Senelick's more recent book-length study, published in 2017, which attributes to Offenbach no less than 'the making of modern culture'.[9] Hungarian secondary literature about Offenbach did not exist, however, until my own study was published in 2021.[10] Until then, the only available publication concerning the subject was a translation of the composer's American travel notes,[11] published long ago in 1960.[12]

The lack of Hungarian secondary literature is not surprising. In the long run, Offenbach and operetta represents all that has traditionally been regarded by some Hungarians as 'unnational' in the history of their country: the study of his fortunes necessarily recalls the practice of German-speaking theatre in the nineteenth century, as well as the history of local German-speaking and Jewish populations – also including the memory of the Holocaust.

Hence, as a research fellow of the Budapest Institute for Musicology, I began my research by studying a huge corpus of performance materials used in Budapest operetta performances between 1859 and 1956, now mainly kept at the Music and Theatre Department of the Széchényi National Library (abbreviated as H-Bn in the footnotes of this Element), and partly in other local libraries and public collections (for a detailed list, see the Acknowledgements). Then, the next step was the study of the local press reception of Offenbach's pieces.

During the research, I not only systematized the extant musico-theatrical sources, performance data, and press reviews, but also attempted to identify

---

[7] Rainer Franke (ed.), *Offenbach und die Schauplätze seines Musiktheaters* (Laaber: Laaber-Verlag, 1999), 10.

[8] Jean-Claude Yon, 'La carrière posthume d'un musicien ou Offenbach aux enfers', *Histoire, économie et société* 22/2 (2003), 261–73.

[9] Laurence Senelick, *Jacques Offenbach and the Making of Modern Culture* (Cambridge: Cambridge University Press, 2017).

[10] Péter Bozó, *Fejezetek Jacques Offenbach magyarországi fogadtatásának történetéből* [Chapters from the history of Jacques Offenbach's Hungarian reception] (Budapest: Rózsavölgyi és Társa Kiadó, 2021).

[11] Offenbach, *Egy muzsikus útinaplója: Offenbach Amerikában* [The travel diary of a musician: Offenbach in America], trans. by Mária Peterdi, introduction by Sándor Fischer (Budapest: Zeneműkiadó, 1960).

[12] Jacques Offenbach, *Offenbach en Amérique: Note d'un musicien en voyage, précédée d'une notice biographique par Albert Wolff* (Paris: Calmann Lévy, 1877).

those factors that affected Offenbach's reception in Budapest. One of the major factors proved to be the local tradition of operetta itself. Differences became apparent already in the second half of the nineteenth century when Offenbach's musical stage works first came to Budapest. More often than not, the Hungarian public got to know these pieces in Austro-German or German adaptations, which necessarily changed the character of the works. Budapest translators also adapted the librettos to local circumstances, not to mention the quite usual practice of re-orchestrating the pieces on the basis of piano vocal scores.

This practice is normal in musical theatre and is not limited to operetta (even if there is a significant difference between the adaptation of a composer's own work and the adaptation of an adaptation).[13] However, what happened with Offenbach's pieces in Budapest in the mid-twentieth century differed radically from earlier adaptations. In the age of totalitarianism, two extremes determined the fate of his pieces in musico-theatrical life: first, their public performance was prohibited during the persecution of Jews between 1938 and 1944; second, some of his works were instrumentalized as pseudo-Offenbachian propaganda pieces during the period between 1949 and 1956. Since both antisemitism and Stalinism exerted a significant influence on Offenbach's Budapest reception, it was the period between the beginning of the Horthy era (1920) and the end of the Rákosi regime (1956) that was chosen as the subject of the present study.

The fundamental thesis of this work is that the difference between the Lyons and Budapest performances of *Orphée* was not merely in the quality of the productions and performers (although it is beyond doubt that there can be radical differences between the staging of the same work by an opera house company and a spoken-word theatre). It is more likely that what happened with Offenbach between 1920 and 1956 still affects the fate of his works in Budapest today. As it was plainly and frankly put by one of the workers at the Budapest Operetta Theatre in 2013: 'Offenbach's pieces are unpopular among the local public these days.' In discussing their performances during the period in question, the primary goal of the two main parts of this study is to show how and why the meaning and connotation of his works changed in such a radical way in Hungary.

2 Offenbach's Reception in Budapest before 1920

It should be emphasized that Offenbach performances in Budapest began well before 1920. His operettas were a brand-new sensation when his first

---

[13] See Hilary Poriss, *Changing the Score: Arias, Prima Donnas, and the Authority of Performance* (Oxford: Oxford University Press, 2009).

pieces arrived in the Hungarian capital just four years after the establishment of the Théâtre des Bouffes-Parisiens. According to the contemporary press, it was in the summer of 1859 that Carl Treumann, a German actor and stage manager of the Vienna Carl-Theater, gave a guest performance at the Buda Arena (see Figure 1).[14] He appeared on the scene in three one-act operettas by Offenbach, first as Peter in *Hochzeit bei Laternenschein* (a role called Guillot in the French original).[15] The following summer all three pieces were revived, and two more one-acters were premiered with Treumann's assistance, partly on the same stage (abbreviated as BA in Table 1) and partly at the Pester Stadttheater (abbreviated as PS).[16]

It is highly typical of local circumstances that the first operettas performed in Budapest were not original works but Viennese adaptations, at least partly in Carl Binder's orchestration, performed by German-speaking artists in a German theatre.[17] Theatrical traditions and audiences in Budapest (which, until 1873, was in fact three separate cities, Buda, Óbuda, and Pest) differed so significantly from those in Paris that a discussion of local Offenbach performances must start with these fundamental differences.

Second Empire Paris was a capital of European theatre and opera. Its operatic life flourished in several institutions dedicated to various genres.[18] Historical *grands opéras* in four or five acts, shorter works called *petits-opéras*, and ballets were performed at the Opéra; Italian opera was the domain of the Théâtre-Italien; reformist pieces were provided at the Théâtre Lyrique, founded in 1847; and the home of *opéras-comiques*, which intermingled vocal numbers and spoken dialogue, was the Théâtre de l'Opéra-Comique. Musical interpolations played a significant role, even

---

[14] According to the playbill reproduced in Figure 1, the venue of the performance was the Pester Stadttheater; however, going by the review published in the same journal, it turns out that the premiere took place at the Buda Arena.

[15] *Pesth-Ofner Localblatt* 10/120 (26 May 1859), [1]; 10/125 (1 June 1859), [2].; 10/130 (8 June 1859), [4].

[16] *Pesth-Ofner Localblatt* 11/140 (16 June 1860), [2]; 11/151 (3 July 1860), [1].

[17] For Offenbach in Vienna, see Walter Obermaier, 'Offenbach in Wien: Seine Werke auf den Vorstadtbühnen und ihr Einfluß auf das Volkstheater', in *Offenbach und die Schauplätze seines Musiktheaters*, ed. by Rainer Franke (Laaber: Laaber-Verlag, 1999), 11–30; Matthias Spohr, 'Inwieweit haben Offenbachs Operetten die Wiener Operette aus der Taufe gehoben?', in *Offenbach und die Schauplätze seines Musiktheaters*, ed. Franke, 31–68; Marion Linhardt, 'Offenbach und die französische Operette im Spiegel der zeitgenössischen Wiener Presse', in *Offenbach und die Schauplätze seines Musiktheaters*, ed. Franke, 69–84; and Rainer Franke, 'Chronologie der Aufführungen der Bühnenwerke Offenbachs in Wien, 1858–1900: Programme, Statistiken, Rezensionen', in *Offenbach und die Schauplätze seines Musiktheaters*, ed. Franke, 119–82.

[18] For Offenbach and the nineteenth-century Parisian theatrical landscape, see Matthias Brzoska, 'Jacques Offenbach und die Operngattungen seiner Zeit', in *Jacques Offenbach und seine Zeit*, ed. by Elisabeth Schmierer (Laaber: Laaber-Verlag, 2009), 27–36.

Figure 1 Playbill of the first known Offenbach performance in Budapest from the *Pesth-Ofner Localblatt* (24 May 1859)

at the institutions dedicated to vaudeville and theatrical plays. In a centre like this, it is not surprising that Offenbach became a theatrical musician. It *is* rather surprising that his theatrical activity did not primarily focus on the

Table 1 Carl Treumann's guest performances, 1859–60

Premiere	Role	Piece	Original title
24 May 1859, BA	Peter	*Hochzeit bei Laternenschein*	*Le mariage aux lanternes*
30 May 1859, BA	Vertigo	*Das Mädchen von Elisonzo*	*Pépito*
6 June 1859, BA	Mathieu	*Die Zaubergeige*	*Le violoneux*
16 June 1860, BA	Isidor	*Der Ehemann vor der Türe*	*Un mari à la porte*
29 June 1860, PS	François	*Die Savoyarden*	*Le 66*

state-subsidized opera houses. Nevertheless, the French traditions of *opéra-comique*,[19] vaudeville,[20] and opera parody[21] played a significant role in the formation of his new genre, described in Central Europe using the umbrella term *Operette*.

In contrast to Paris, nineteenth-century Budapest was a city of only local importance from a theatrical perspective. As Hungary was part of the Habsburg Empire, the residential city of the ruler was Vienna, hence there was no opera house in Budapest until 1884. The other decisive factor that formed the character of theatrical life was the multi-ethnic character of the capital, which differed significantly from the cosmopolitan internationalism of Paris. As the Hungarian statistician Elek Fényes wrote in 1851, 'the most numerous are the Germans,

---

[19] See Offenbach's overview of the history of *opéra-comique*, written on the occasion of an operetta-writing competition organized by the Théâtre des Bouffes-Parisiens: Jacques Offenbach, 'Concours pour une opérette en un acte', *La France Musicale* 3/148 (17 July 1856), 6–7. For the theatrical context of this manifesto, see Mark Everist, 'Jacques Offenbach: The Music of the Past and the Image of the Present', in *Music, Theater, and Cultural Transfer: Paris, 1830–1914*, ed. by Mark Everist and Annegret Fauser (Chicago: The University of Chicago Press, 2009), 72–98; republished in Mark Everist, *Opera in Paris from the Empire to the Commune* (New York: Routledge, 2019).

[20] For Offenbach and vaudeville, see Ralf-Olivier Schwarz, *Vaudeville und Operette: Jacques Offenbach's Werke für das Théâtre du Palais-Royal* (Fernwald: Burkhard Muth, 2007); Schwarz, 'Vom Witz des Vaudevilles zum Rausch der Operette: *La Vie parisienne*', in *Jacques Offenbach und seine Zeit*, ed. Schmierer, 198–220; Schwarz, '"Es ist das lustigste Theater in Paris": Musik und Bühne am Théâtre du Palais-Royal 1831–1866', in *Jacques Offenbach und seine Zeit*, ed. Schmierer, 46–64.

[21] For Offenbach and opera parody, see Siegfried Dörffeldt, 'Die musikalische Parodie bei Offenbach' (PhD diss., Johann-Wolfgang-Goethe-Universität, 1954) and Péter Bozó, 'Offenbach and the Representation of the Salon', in *Musical Salon Culture in the Long Nineteenth Century*, ed. by Anja Bunzel and Natasha Loges (Woodbridge: The Boydell Press, 2019), 139–52.

then the Hungarians; much less the Slovaks and Serbs; although there are hardly any inhabitants in Pest who cannot speak or at least understand German and Hungarian at the same time'.[22] Fényes obviously based his claim on the results of the 1851 census, according to which, of the whole population of the capital (107,334 persons), 33,951 were native German speakers (31.63 per cent) and 32,562 native Hungarians (30.33 per cent).[23] Three decades later, according to the 1881 census, in Pest the number of Hungarian speakers (58.98 per cent) already exceeded that of Germans (28.8 per cent). In Buda, however, there was a German majority even at that time (50.21 per cent Germans and 40.46 per cent Hungarians), just like Óbuda (62 per cent Germans).[24]

Under such circumstances, the main difference between local theatres was not the genre they cultivated but their language. At the time when Offenbach's first operettas were premiered, German performances were given in three places: the Pest Municipal Theatre, the Buda Municipal Theatre, and the Buda Arena.[25] Until 1861, the only Hungarian theatre was the state-subsidized Pest National Theatre.[26] All three German stages belonged to one institution called the Vereinigte Deutsche Theater, directed by Georg Gundy in 1859–60.[27] Both the national and the German theatres provided all kinds of spectacles, produced on the same stage and more or less by the same company: operas, ballets, spoken-word plays, and other entertaining repertoire.

At the beginning of the 1860s, some changes in the theatrical landscape took place: on 26 August 1860 a German entrepreneur, Carl Alsdorf, opened a new German summer stage called the Thalia Theatre in the Budapest City Park (Városliget/Stadtwäldchen). It is worth mentioning that on the occasion of the opening performance of the new institution, two of the operettas premiered by Treumann were performed by local theatre companies: *Die Zaubergeige* and *Hochzeit bei Laternenschein*, attesting to the success of Offenbach's works.[28]

---

[22] Elek Fényes, *Magyarország geographiai szótára, mellyben minden város, falu és puszta, betűrendben, körülményesen leiratik* [Geographical dictionary of Hungary, in which every city, village, and wilderness is circumstantially described in alphabetical order], vol. 3 (Pest: Kozma Vazul, 1851), 224.

[23] József Kőrösi (ed.), *Budapest fővárosa az 1881. évben* [The capital Budapest in 1881] (Budapest: Ráth Mór, 1882), 110.

[24] Ibid., 101–5.

[25] For German theatre-making in Budapest, see Wolfgang Binal, *Deutschsprachiges Theater in Budapest* (Vienna: Böhlaus Nachfolger, 1972).

[26] For the history of nineteenth-century Hungarian theatre-making, see Ferenc Kerényi (ed.), *Magyar színháztörténet*, vol. 1: *1790–1873* (Budapest: Magyar Színházi Intézet, 1990); Tamás Gajdó (ed.), vol. 2: *1873–1920* (Budapest: Magyar Könyvklub/OSZMI, 2001).

[27] L. Schneider (ed.), *Deutscher Bühnen-Almanach*, vol. 24 (Berlin: Hayn, 1860), 317.

[28] N. N., 'Die Eröffnung des Thalia-Theaters', *Pesth-Ofner Localblatt* 11/197 (28 August 1860), [3].

Table 2 Offenbach at the Buda Folk Theatre, 1861–70

Premiere	Piece	Original title
24 Sept. 1861	*Férj az ajtó előtt*	*Un Mari à la porte*
11 June 1862	*Daphnis és Chloé*	*Daphnis et Chloé*
17 Jan. 1863	*Dunanan apó és fia utazása*	*Le Voyage de MM. Dunanan père et fils*
28 Feb. 1863	*A dajka*	*La Bonne d'enfant*
18 Apr. 1863	*Choufleuri úr otthon lesz*	*M. Choufleuri restera chez lui le . . .*
3 Oct. 1863	*A kofák*	*Mesdames de la Halle*
24 Oct. 1863	*A fecsegők*	*Les Bavards*
7 Nov. 1863	*A 66. Szám*	*Le 66*
5 Mar. 1864	*Vasgyúró, a legislegutolsó lovag*	*Croquefer ou Le Dernier des paladins*
11 May 1864	*Genovéva*	*Geneviève de Brabant*
13 Aug. 1864	*A georgiai nők*	*Les Géorgiennes*
11 Oct. 1867	*A gerolsteini nagyhercegnő*	*La Grande-Duchesse de Gérolstein*
18 Nov. 1868	*A makaróniárus*	*Coscoletto, ou le lazarone*

Another important event in 1860 was the appearance of a new Hungarian company in the capital, led by György Molnár. At first, it shared the stage of the Buda Arena with the Germans, but from 1861 on the company performed at a new, second Hungarian institution called the Buda Folk Theatre (Budai Népszínház). Although Molnár's enterprise proved to be short-lived – it went bankrupt after two short cycles (1861–4 and 1867–70) – it represented an important new trend in local theatre-making. It was the first attempt to dedicate a separate stage to the popular repertoire, including Offenbach's operettas (see Table 2). It is also worth mentioning that Molnár received at least some of the performing materials directly from Paris.[29] Although the performance practice at his theatre is not well documented, one can presume that the pieces staged there were closer in approach to the French practice than those staged at other Hungarian theatres. Furthermore, the above-mentioned changes did not alter the

---

[29] According to contemporary press reports, in Paris he purchased the performing materials for Offenbach's *Mesdames de la Halle*, *Geneviève de Brabant*, *Le 66*, *Les Deux pêcheurs*, *La Rose de Saint-Flour*, *Tromb-al-ca-zar ou Les Criminels dramatiques*, *Croquefer ou Le dernier des paladins*, *Une Nuit blanche*, *Ba-Ta-Clan*, and *Vent-du-soir ou L'horrible festin*. N. N., 'Színházi hírek' [Theatrical news], *Színházi Látcső* 1/51 (27 May 1863), [3]–[4].

Table 3 Offenbach premieres at the Pest National Theatre, 1860–4

Premiere	Piece	Original title
21 Nov. 1860	*Eljegyzés Lámpafénynél*	*Le Mariage aux lanternes*
14 Feb. 1861	*Férj az ajtó előtt*	*Un Mari à la porte*
14 Mar. 1861	*A varázshegedű*	*Le Violoneux*
30 Sep. 1861	*Az elizondói leány*	*Pépito*
25 Jan. 1862	*Fortunio dala*	*La Chanson de Fortunio*
31 July 1862	*Denis úr és neje*	*M. et Mme Denis*
12 Oct. 1863	*Az átváltozott Macska*	*La Chatte métamorphosée en femme*

fact that Budapest theatres at that time belonged to the category of *Mehrspartentheater* in the German secondary literature.

In contemporary Paris, it would have been unimaginable to perform operettas at the Comédie-Française, dedicated as it was to native spoken drama. In Budapest, however, this is exactly what happened at the National Theatre under the intendant Mihály Nyéki. Between November 1860 and October 1863 seven Offenbach one-acters were premiered (see Table 3). The performance materials used came from different sources: the libretto[30] and printed vocal score[31] of *Eljegyzés lámpafénynél* arrived from Berlin; the full score of *A varázshegedű* from Vienna;[32] while *Az átváltozott macska* was played during a guest performance by Pepi (Jozefa) Szabó from Košice in Endre Latabár's Hungarian translation, which was premiered there.[33] What is more, in July 1861, a six-day guest performance by Offenbach's own company took place at the National Theatre (see Table 4).

The mixed repertoire of the institution had strange consequences. Since it was also the home of opera, it was there that in 1863 Richard Wagner conducted two concerts of his own works. Some of the singers participating in the Offenbach performances – for example, the soprano Ilka Markovits and the baritone Károly Kőszeghy – also took part in the first local premieres of Wagner's music dramas, partly under Hans Richter's baton. However, the

---

[30] H-Bn, Theatre Department, MM 18.750.
[31] Kept in the library of the Hungarian State Opera House, without a shelf mark (Bote & Bock's edition). Cf. H-Bn, Theatre Department, Fond 4/96, fol. 2r.
[32] H-Bn, ZBK 204/a.
[33] The Košice premiere took place on 2 November 1862. See the local theatre playbills: H-Bn, Theatre Department (without shelf marks).

Table 4 Guest performances by the Théâtre des Bouffes-Parisiens at the Pest
National Theatre

Date	Piece
12 July 1861	*La Chatte métamorphosée en femme*
	Mesdames de la Halle
13 July 1861	*La Chanson de Fortunio*
	Une Demoiselle en lôterie
14 July 1861	*Une Mari à la porte*
16 July 1861	*Orphée aux enfers*
17 July 1861	*La Chanson de Fortunio*
18 July 1861	*Les Ponts des Soupirs*

factotum of the Offenbach operettas was Kálmán Szerdahelyi, a gifted comic
actor but a poor singer, who appeared mostly in spoken drama. He not only
played leading roles but was also the translator of the libretto in three cases, and
the stage manager (SM) of four productions (see Table 5).

Since both Offenbach's and Wagner's performances took place at the
National Theatre, press reviews did not hesitate to measure the two composers
against each other.[34] In 1866, following the Pest premiere of Wagner's
Lohengrin, Kornél Ábrányi, editor-in-chief of the music magazine *Zenészeti
lapok*, wrote the following:

> Frequently, the objection to Wagner's music is that there are very few
> melodies in it, [so] it is incomprehensible, music just for connoisseurs, and
> what is more for the cream of music connoisseurs. Those who talk that way
> are seeking a reason without finding it. For if people hear out this opera
> attentively and are only to some degree musical connoisseurs, or merely
> have some affinity for music, they must recognize on the contrary that
> there are too many melodies in Wagner, if not in the same sense as the word
> 'melody' can be used in connection with Italian operas or Offenbach's
> operettas.[35]

---

[34] For more on Wagner and Offenbach in a wider European context, see Flora Willson, 'Future
History: Wagner, Offenbach, and "la musique de l'avenir" in Paris, 1860', *Opera Quarterly* 30/4
(2014), 287–314; Peter Mondelli, 'Offenbach's *Bouffonnerie*, Wagner's *Rêverie*: The
Materiality and Politics of the Ineffable in Second Empire Paris', *Opera Quarterly* 32/2–3
(2016), 134–59; Peter Ackermann, 'Eine Kapitulation: zum Verhältnis Offenbach–Wagner', in
Jacques Offenbach: Komponist und Weltbürger, ed. by Winfried Kirsch und Ronny Dietrich
(Mainz: Schott's Söhne, 1985), 135–48.

[35] '[Á]k', 'Lohengrin: Regényes dalmű három felvonásban' [*Lohengrin:* Romantic opera in three
acts], *Zenészeti Lapok* 7/11 (16 December 1866), 164.

Table 5 Markovits's, Kőszeghy's, and Szerdahelyi's roles in Offenbach and
Wagner premieres

Piece	Markovits	Kőszeghy	Szerdahelyi
Eljegyzés lámpafénynél	Katalin	–	Péter
Férj az ajtó előtt	Zsuzsanna	Trompeur Márton	Ducroquet Flórián; trans., SM
A varázshegedű	Antal	–	Mathieu; trans., SM
Az elizondói leány	Manuelita	Vertigo	–
Fortunio dala	Bálint	–	Fortunio; SM
Denis úr és neje	Nanette	–	trans.
Az átváltozott macska	–	Dig-Dig	Guido, SM
Lohengrin (first perf. 1 Nov. 1866)	–	Madarász Henrik	–
Tannhäuser (first perf. 11 March 1871)	Erzsébet	–	–
A bolygó hollandi [*Der fliegende Holländer*] (first perf. 10 May 1873)	–	Daland	–
Rienzi (first perf. 24 Nov. 1874)	–	Cecco	–

It is worth noting that Ábrányi was a Wagner propagandist, and from his few
sentences it is clear that he sought to render Wagner's music understandable and
acceptable to Pest audiences of the time. Yet the paragraph reveals something not
only of Ábrányi's relation to Wagner but of the place Offenbach held in the
system of values at the time. To Ábrányi, Offenbach's music represents the polar
opposite of Wagner's but stands concurrently on the same level as Italian opera.

Ábrányi's equation of Offenbach's operettas and Italian operas might surprise
present-day musicologists, as post-Offenbach operetta in the twentieth century
moved in a commercially popular direction. Thus, the term 'operetta' today no
longer means a subgenre of opera, but a separate genre distinct from opera.
However, in the mid-nineteenth century, particularly before the European
dissemination of Offenbach's works, operetta was seen as such a subgenre:
a musical stage work in which spoken dialogue replaced recitative. The very

term for it betrays that meaning, in a way well documented by Sabine Ehrmann-Herforth, who quotes widely from music dictionaries of the seventeenth-to-twentieth centuries.[36]

Six years after the *Lohengrin* review, when Offenbach again came to Budapest in 1872 and conducted the local premiere of his *opéra bouffe Schneeball* (*Boule-de-neige*) at the Deutsches Theater in der Wollgasse, he attended a performance of Wagner's *Tannhäuser* at the National Theatre. The daily newspaper *Fővárosi Lapok* reported on the event in the following way:

> The *Tannhäuser* performance last Saturday was in many ways more superb than any so far. . . . This time we saw the Pest *haute creme* in the boxes. In one ground floor box sat Offenbach, the prolific operetta composer. The butterfly visited the lion, but could not stand the lion's great voice for long: he heard only one and a half acts of Wagner's music, which marks the polar opposite of his in the music world.[37]

It can be objected that the press reports quoted are just examples taken out of context, but in fact there are further cases of the names Wagner and Offenbach being attached in music reviews in nineteenth-century Budapest. To take another, later example: a quarter-century after the *Lohengrin* premiere, in 1890, a review appeared in the music magazine *Zenelap* of the first performance of Offenbach's *Le Mariage aux lanternes* at the Budapest Royal Opera House. The anonymous author heavily criticized the programming of Gustav Mahler, who was music director there between 1888 and 1891:

> It is nice of him [i.e., Mahler] to introduce every subgenre of opera into our Opera House – as we have only one Opera House, and so cannot separate the different operatic genres. But he should not go so far as to introduce Offenbach's operettas into the home of the serious Muse, as it is reputed to

---

[36] Sabine Ehrmann-Herfort, 'Operette', in *Handwörterbuch der musikalischen Terminologie*, ed. by Albrecht Riethmüller, vol. 4 (Stuttgart: Steiner, 1972), 1–20.

[37] N. N., 'Fővárosi hírek' [News from the capital], *Fővárosi Lapok* 9/92 (23 April 1872), 399. Here the animal metaphor used by the anonymous author – for whom Offenbach was evidently the polar opposite of Wagner – is suspiciously similar to one used by Robert Schumann in his recounting of a Rossini encounter with Beethoven; see Robert Schumann, *On Music and Musicians*, ed. by Konrad Wolff, trans. by Paul Rosenfeld (Berkeley and Los Angeles: University of California Press, 1983), 235. A collected edition of Schumann's music reviews was published in 1854, so the author of the press review might have known Schumann's aphorism. See Robert Schumann, *Gesammelte Schriften über Musik und Musiker* (Leipzig: Wigand, 1854), vol. 1, 210. For the subject of *Stildualismus*, see Carl Dahlhaus, *Nineteenth-Century Music*, trans. by J. Bradford Robinson (Berkeley and Los Angeles: University of California Press, 1989), 8–15; Benjamin Walton, *Rossini in Restoration Paris: The Sound of Modern Life* (Cambridge: Cambridge University Press, 2007), 210–56; Nicholas Mathew and Benjamin Walton (eds.), *The Invention of Beethoven and Rossini: Historiography, Analysis, Criticism* (Cambridge: Cambridge University Press, 2013).

be. We salute Wagner's music with holy horror and listen to it, just not too much, and we also would like to hear Kreutzer's poetic and heartbreaking songs, and the witty and fresh music of the Frenchman, and the Hungarian character of our Royal Opera House should be conserved through the cultivation of the works by Hungarian composers.[38]

In contrast to Ábrányi's review, Offenbach and Wagner are mentioned here as two composers falling into the same category, neither being too desirable on the Opera House stage. Wagner's music is graded somewhat better and could be allowed, if not too often and if saluted 'with holy horror'; but performing Offenbach there is condemned out of hand. Yet the strongest remark in the quotation is its last sentence, and the national bias is still more emphatic because the complete review begins thus: 'One and a half years went by and no Hungarian opera was played at the Royal Hungarian Opera House.'[39] That, by the way, is untrue: to provide one example, Erkel's opera *György Brankovics* was revived there in February 1890. Under these circumstances, it is clear that the critic was biased against Mahler, and in that context, it is unsurprising that the two foreign composers he programmed should be condemned equally. More surprising is that Conradin Kreutzer, a minor German composer whose romantic opera *Das Nachtlager in Granada* was premiered in Budapest under Mahler's directorship, is given a positive note.[40]

Despite its brevity, Mahler's activity as artistic director (1888–91) marked a flourishing period in the history of the Budapest Opera House, with such important local premieres as Wagner's *Das Rheingold* and *Die Walküre* (1889), and *Cavalleria rusticana* by Mascagni (1890). Of Offenbach's pieces,[41] he planned to programme a cycle of one-acters comprising *La Chanson de Fortunio*, *Le Mariage aux lanternes*, and *Le Violoneux*,[42] as well as *Les Contes d'Hoffmann*,[43] with the soprano Bianca Bianchi (Bertha Schwarz) in the leading female roles.[44] Bianchi, however, fell ill, and only the premiere of *Le*

---

[38] N. N., 'A m[agyar] kir[ályi] operaház, a magyar opera és még egyéb' [The Hungarian Royal Opera House, Hungarian opera and other things], *Zenészeti Lapok* 5/3 (30 January 1890), 2.

[39] Ibid., 1.

[40] For the negative attitude of the contemporary Hungarian press towards Mahler, see Markian Prokopovych, 'Stylistic Challenge, 1889: Gustav Mahler and the International Operetta', in Prokopovych, *In the Public Eye: The Budapest Opera House, the Audience and the Press, 1884–1918* (Vienna: Böhlau Verlag, 2014), 127–47.

[41] For Mahler's attitude to Offenbach, see Lóránt Péteri, 'Idyllic Masks of Death: References to *Orphée aux Enfers* in "Das himmlische Leben"', in *Rethinking Mahler*, ed. by Jeremy Barham (New York: Oxford University Press, 2017), 127–37.

[42] 'N. N.', 'Mahler programmja' [Mahler's programme] *Budapesti Hírlap* 9/273 (4 October 1889), 4.

[43] 'N. N.', 'Színház, zene, képzőművészet' [Theatre, music, fine arts] *Pesti Hírlap* 12/251 (12 September 1890), 4.

[44] 'N. N.', 'Színház, zene, képzőművészet' [Theatre, music, fine arts], *Pesti Hírlap* 12/163 (15 June 1890), 4.

Mariage aux lanternes took place, without her participation or Mahler's conductorship. Even the premiere of *Les Contes* was postponed, and then, when Mahler resigned from his post, was cancelled.[45]

In Budapest at that time, Offenbach's posthumous opera belonged to the popular repertoire of the Folk Theatre (Népszínház), along with several other of Offenbach's *opérettes* and *opéras bouffes*. Opened in 1875 and operating until 1908, this institution was destined to promote the folk plays and operettas that had been performed earlier at the National Theatre. Beside its popular character, the Folk Theatre also had an ideological, 'nation-building' function: the dissemination of Hungarian language and culture. Its first director was Jenő Rákosi, an assimilated *Ungarndeutsch*, who promoted Hungarian nationalism with a neophyte fervour as the editor-in-chief of the daily newspaper *Budapesti Hírlap*.[46] Strangely enough, it was in this theatre that the Hungarian premiere of *Les Contes d'Hoffmann* took place on 14 April 1882, performed and designated on the playbills as an operetta. It featured spoken dialogue, starred the Roma operetta prima donna Aranka Hegyi, and, at first, was performed without the Giulietta act.[47] (The latter also premiered there on 12 January 1883, but did not prove successful; it had only two performances.)

Mahler's plan to include *Les Contes d'Hoffmann* in the repertoire of the Opera House with Bianchi in the leading female roles would only be realized ten years after he left Budapest, on 15 December 1900. The work was performed with recitatives and with the Giulietta act; this time, however, Stella and Lindorf were missing from the playbills since both the prologue and the epilogue of the piece were heavily cut[48] – a quite usual practice in early German-language performances of the opera.[49] The work was well received but proved to be not outstandingly successful. In this respect, the real breakthrough happened in 1913, when it was successfully revived at the Opera House on 19 January with Erzsi Sándor in the leading female roles and with full-length prologue and epilogue. According to the press reviews, the *mise en scène* by Sándor Hevesi, as well as the costumes and stage sets by Count Miklós Bánffy, significantly

[45] 'N. N.', 'Ferenc Beniczky', *Budapesti Hírlap* 11/25 (25 January 1891), 9.

[46] János Gyurgyák, *Ezzé lett magyar hazátok: A magyar nemzeteszme és nacionalizmus története* [Your Hungarian homeland became like this: A history of Hungarian nationalism] (Budapest: Osiris Kiadó, 2007), 101–4.

[47] For the premiere at the Vienna Ringtheater, the work was also designated as a 'fantastische Operette'. See Obermaier, 'Offenbach in Wien', 29.

[48] As is revealed by a printed copy of the libretto (Budapest: Müller Károly, 1900), translated by Antal Várady, Jakab Béla Fái, and Antal Radó: H-Bn, Central Collection, 820.502.

[49] Arne Langer, 'Die Eröffnungsinszenierung an der Komischen Oper Berlin (1905) im Kontext der Editions- und Aufführungsgeschichte von *Hoffmanns Erzählungen* (1905) im deutschsprachigen Raum: Deutschsprachige Erstaufführungen von *Hoffmanns Erzählungen* bis 1905', in *Offenbach und die Schauplätze*, ed. Franke, 215–56.

contributed to its success.[50] Due to this production, *Les Contes d'Hoffmann* became a repertoire piece of the Opera House, which at the same time meant that Offenbach was regarded as a classical composer in Budapest on the eve of World War I. But what happened with his works thereafter?

3 Offenbach during the Horthy Regime, 1920–1944

Historical Context

With a devastating war, revolution, and counter-revolution as well as the collapse of the Habsburg Empire and of the dual monarchy of Austria–Hungary – the beginning of the period in question was a time of serious social and political conflicts. Only five years after the successful revival of *Les Contes d'Hoffmann* at the Budapest Opera House, World War I ended in 1918 with the complete military defeat of Austria–Hungary and the Central Powers. In addition to significant military casualties, even the hinterland faced serious problems like inflation, a shortage of labour, supply difficulties, and requisitions. While in 1914 most of the populace welcomed the war enthusiastically, by 1918 the enthusiasm had turned to disappointment and discontent.[51]

In October 1918, the democratic opposition parties established a National Council whose president became the left-liberal Count Mihály Károlyi. As a kind of counter-government, the Council sought the immediate termination of the war, national independence, democratic reforms, and reconciliation with ethnic minorities. The Budapest population wanted Károlyi for prime minister, and several demonstrators were shot dead when police tried to disband a throng demanding his appointment. As a response, a revolution broke out and King Charles IV was forced to appoint Károlyi, who proclaimed the Hungarian People's Republic on 16 November. Since protesters placed aster flowers in their hats during the riots, the event received the name 'Aster Revolution'.[52]

Károlyi tried unsuccessfully to remedy social and economic problems, effectuate democratic reforms, and to preserve the integrity of the country and to cease its political isolation. His government was equally opposed by the anti-liberal and antisemitic right-wing movements, by the traditional conservative-liberal elite, and by the newly established Communist Party (KMP).[53] Finally, Károlyi lost his power when on 21 March 1919 the Communists and the Social

---

[50] See among others Aladár Bálint, 'Az Operaház új Hoffmannja' [The new Hoffmann of the Opera House], *Nyugat* 6/3 (1 February 1913), 218–19; Sándor Jeszenszky, 'Hoffmann meséi', *Zeneközlöny* 11/13 (15 February 1913), 437.

[51] Ignác Romsics, *Magyarország története a XX. században* (Budapest: Osiris Kiadó, 2003), 106–7. Romsics's volume can also be read in English: *Hungary in the Twentieth Century* (Budapest: Corvina Kiadó, 2/2010 [1/1999]).

[52] Ibid., 112–14.   [53] Ibid., 115–23.

Democratic Party organized a coup by common accord, declaring the reign of the proletariat and the beginning of the Hungarian Soviet Republic. The new regime radically broke with earlier political traditions. One of its first measures was the abolition of private property; privately owned lands, factories, banks, schools, and universities were nationalized; prices were fixed; and bourgeois newspapers were prohibited. The takeover was accompanied by the so-called 'Red Terror': many people opposing the new regime were killed by József Cserny and his 'Lenin Boys'. The Paris peace conference was surprised by the Communist coup and feared the spread of Bolshevism. Romanian, Czechoslovak, Serb, and French troops embarked on a military intervention, and a great part of Hungary was occupied. Initially, the armed resistance of the Hungarian Red Army was successful. However, by July 1919 Romanian troops gained the advantage and on 1 August the Communist leadership resigned and most of them fled abroad. In the first days of August even the capital was occupied by Romanian soldiers.[54] Under such circumstances, the centenary of Offenbach's birth passed unnoticed.

For a while, the country had no internationally recognized government. The situation changed only in November when the Romanian troops began to withdraw and vice-admiral Miklós Horthy marched into Budapest with his troops. Károly Huszár's new government was dominated by the so-called Christian National Union Party. The new National Assembly was elected in January 1920; in February, the new system of government was also decided. Since the restoration of the Habsburg Monarchy would have been unacceptable not only for the great powers but also for a significant number of local parliamentarians, the country remained a kingdom without king. In March, Miklós Horthy was elected Regent and held this post until 1944, hence becoming the eponym of the era. His authoritarian political regime faced serious problems. In the Trianon Peace Treaty, signed on 4 June 1920, Hungary lost approximately two-thirds of its territory and more than half of its population, and irredentism and revisionism became the main focus of Hungarian foreign policy. Beside national resentment, the war also had serious economic consequences such as unemployment and heavy inflation. However, Offenbach's music and the social criticism in his stage works retained their authenticity even under the changing social circumstances, as is attested by the successful revival of *Orphée aux enfers* at the Buda Summer Arena on 3 July 1920.[55]

Given Offenbach's Jewish background (even though he converted to Catholicism in 1844), his reception during this era should be understood in

---

[54] Ibid., 123–32.
[55] 'N. N.', 'Színház és zene' [Music and theatre], *Budapesti Hírlap* 40/168 (16 July 1920), 4.

the context of the time. Antisemitism was part of the public discourse and legislation of the Horthy era right from the beginning.[56] The takeover was accompanied by the so-called 'White Terror': many people were killed, among them not only supporters of the Soviet Republic but also Jewish citizens who had nothing to do with the Communist regime. As early as 1920, the *numerus clausus* law was adopted by the National Assembly.[57] This law introduced a mechanism to keep Jews out of universities by screening all applicants as to whether or not they were Jewish, either by religion or by birth. The measure seriously affected people living in Budapest since, according to the results of the 1920 census, of the population of 930,247 no less than 212,736 inhabitants (22.9 per cent) were Jewish.[58] (This figure does not include those Jews who had converted to other religions.)

However, there were significant differences in the character and measure of antisemitism during the period. Following the rise of virulent antisemitism and increase in the number of antisemitic incidents in and around 1920, prime minister István Bethlen successfully consolidated the internal politics of Hungary between 1921 and 1931, so much so that the situation of the Hungarian Jewish community improved significantly in the second half of the 1920s.[59] Even the overtly discriminatory part of the *numerus clausus* law was amended in 1928 in response to international protests.[60] The fact that in 1933 it was possible to perform Offenbach's *Les Brigands* as *A banditák* on the stage of the Budapest Opera House should be interpreted in the context of these developments.

Nevertheless, this more peaceful period proved to be temporary, and things began to change following the Great Depression in 1929. In contrast to Bethlen, his successor, Gyula Gömbös (prime minister between 1932 and 1936) belonged to the so-called *fajvédő* (race-protection) movement, an antisemitic wing of the far right.[61] Although there was no discriminatory legislation enacted

---

[56] About Jews and antisemitism in the Horthy Era, see János Gyurgyák, *A zsidókérdés Magyarországon* [The 'Jewish question' in Hungary] (Budapest: Osiris Kiadó, 2001), 197–208; see also Ignác Romsics, *A Horthy-korszak* [The Horthy era] (Budapest: Helikon Kiadó, 2017), 333–48.

[57] For this law, see *The Numerus Clausus in Hungary: Studies on the First Anti-Jewish Law and Academic Anti-Semitism in Modern Central Europe*, ed. by Victor Karady and Péter Tibor Nagy (Budapest: Pasts Inc. Centre for Historical Research, History Department of the Central European University, 2012).

[58] *Budapest székesfőváros statisztikai közleményei*, vol. 52: *Az 1920. évi népszámlálás előzetes eredményei* [Statistical Publications of the Capital City Budapest, vol. 52: Preliminary Results of the 1920 Census], ed. by Gusztáv Thirring (Budapest: Budapest Székesfőváros Statisztikai Hivatala, 1921), 10 and 12.

[59] Gyurgyák, *A zsidókérdés*, 123–31.   [60] Ibid.

[61] About the race-protection movement, see János Gyurgyák, *Magyar fajvédők* [Hungarian race-protectionists] (Budapest: Osiris, 2012).

during his governance, significant changes in the political elite took place at that time: Gömbös's comrades in the Race-Protection Party came to the fore. After 1933, when Adolf Hitler attained power in Berlin, German influence became stronger.[62]

The year 1938 proved to be a watershed both in European and Hungarian politics. Following the *Anschluss*, when Nazi Germany annexed Austria (12 March 1938), anti-Jewish legislation also began to be enacted in Hungary. The so-called 'First Jewish Law' (29 May 1938) restricted the proportion of Jews to 20 per cent in several (mainly intellectual) professions.[63] The 'Second Jewish Law' (5 May 1939) defined Jews racially for the first time: people with at least two Jewish-born grandparents were declared Jews.[64] Finally, the 'Third Jewish Law' (8 August 1941), passed under prime minister László Bárdossy, prohibited marriage and penalized sexual intercourse between Jews and non-Jews.[65] On 16 April 1941, the armed military service of 'politically unreliable' Jewish men was prohibited, obliging them to serve in the so-called 'labour service', which effectively meant forced labour.[66] On 30 April 1944, works by 144 Hungarian and 34 foreign Jewish authors were put on the index of banned publications; a second *index librorum prohibitorum* appeared on 24 June of the same year containing the names of 127 Hungarian and 11 foreign authors.[67] The books prohibited were destroyed publicly. Although Offenbach's name did not figure on the list, there was no question that his works were undesirable. In 1940, when the company of the Capital City Gaiety Theatre were planning to perform *La Belle Hélène* on the Margaret Island Open-Air Stage, all open-air performances were proscribed by the government.[68]

Finally, it would be the German occupation of Hungary on 19 March 1944 that irrevocably decided the fate of the Hungarian Jews.[69] The country became Hitler's puppet state, and Döme Sztójay's government began to execute the programme of the Nazi *Endlösung*. Between 14 May and 9 July 1944, when Regent Horthy stopped the deportations following international protests, at least 450,000 Jews were deported with the active assistance of the Hungarian authorities to German concentration camps, where most of them were killed.[70] Following Horthy's unsuccessful attempt to take Hungary out of the Axis alliance, on 15 October 1944 the Regent was taken into detention by German

---

[62] Gyurgyák, *A zsidókérdés*, 131–5.   [63] Ibid., 135–42.   [64] Ibid., 143–52.   [65] Ibid., 153–8.
[66] Ibid., 170–1.   [67] Ibid., 178–79.
[68] '(–or)', 'Színház és zene' [Music and theatre], *Pesti Hírlap* 42/151 (6 July 1940), 9.
[69] For a detailed survey of the Hungarian Holocaust, see Randolph L. Braham, *A népirtás politikája: A holocaust Magyarországon*, trans. Tamás Zala (Budapest: Belvárosi Könyvkiadó, 1997); in English: *The Politics of Genocide: The Holocaust in Hungary* (New York: Columbia University Press, 3/2016 [1/1981]).
[70] Braham, *A népirtás politikája*, 180.

soldiers and forced to resign. As a consequence of the coup, the 'Leader of the Nation' became Ferenc Szálasi, the head of the extreme right-wing Arrow Cross Party. During the pogroms that took place under his reign of terror, further tens of thousands of Jews living in Budapest were killed. According to Romsics, approximately 600,000 Hungarian civilians were killed during World War II, and most of them (almost 500,000) were of Jewish descent.[71]

Theatrical Context: Operetta in Hungary during the Interwar Period and World War II

Around 1920, the circumstances under which Offenbach's pieces were performed in Budapest had significantly changed from those during his life or in the last years of the nineteenth century. By then, not only had the concept of 'serious music' had changed but even entertaining musical theatre had been significantly transformed. By the end of World War I, Budapest had already seen not only the beginnings of Béla Bartók's, Zoltán Kodály's, and Ernst von Dohnányi's compositional careers, but also the premiere of Emmerich Kálmán's *Die Csárdásfürstin* (2 November 1916) and Albert Szirmai's *Mágnás Miska* (12 February 1916).[72] What is more, according to Richard Traubner, after World War I Budapest 'joined the list of principal operetta cities' alongside Berlin and New York.[73] As will be shown in the next section, the flourishing of the native operetta school had a strong impact on local Offenbach performances.

The theatrical landscape of the capital also changed at the beginning of the twentieth century. At the turn of the century, a private theatrical industry came into existence whose products proved to be successful and even exportable. The Folk Theatre was unable to compete with the new private theatres, the Gaiety Theatre (Vígszínház), founded in 1896, the Hungarian Theatre (Magyar Színház), opened in 1897, and the Király Theatre (Király Színház), established in 1903. In the face of this competition, the Folk Theatre finally ceased to exist in 1908, after Raoul Mader, former conductor and director of the Opera House, had unsuccessfully tried to resuscitate it as the Comic Opera (Népszínház-Vígopera). The Folk Opera (Népopera) founded in 1911 by the Márkus family and competing with the Opera House was quite similar to Mader's enterprise.[74] It cultivated both serious and light musico-theatrical genres: the two poles of its repertoire can be exemplified by such works as

---

[71] Romsics, *A Horthy-korszak*, 346.

[72] For a short overview of operetta in Hungary, see Lynn M. Hooker, 'Hungarians and Hungarianisms in Operetta', in *The Cambridge Companion to Operetta*, ed. by Anastasia Belina and Derek B. Scott (Cambridge: Cambridge University Press, 2020), 61–75.

[73] Richard Traubner, *Operetta: A Theatrical History* (New York: Routledge, 2/2003 [1/1980]), viii.

[74] Tibor Tallián, 'Népoperai kezdeményezések a századelő Budapestjén' [Popular operatic enterprises in turn-of-the-century Budapest], *Muzsika* 40/10 (October 1997), 13–16.

Wagner's *Parsifal* (first Hungarian performance, 1 January 1914) and István Gajáry's operetta *Böském* (14 March 1914).[75] Even Offenbach's *Les Contes d'Hoffmann* was regularly staged there, for the first time on 7 September 1912 with Adelina Adler in the leading female roles.[76] The Folk Opera went bankrupt in 1915 and its building became the property of the capital city. It was renamed the Municipal Theatre in 1917.

Evidently, World War I also affected the theatrical entertainment industry, which tried to overcome its financial difficulties through mergers and acquisitions.[77] Established in 1918, the Union Theatre Operations and Building Ltd. (Unió Színházüzemi és Színházépítő Részvénytársaság) comprised at first the Hungarian and the Király Theatres.[78] However, in 1920 it also acquired the City Centre Theatre (Belvárosi Színház), while later, in 1921, it also purchased the Andrássy Street Theatre (Andrássy Úti Színház) and the Lujza Blaha Theatre (Blaha Lujza Színház). In 1922, a new institution for operetta performances was even established: the Capital City Operetta Theatre (Fővárosi Operettszínház). The privileged role of the Rákosi family did not change; until 1924, László Beöthy, the nephew of the first director of the Folk Theatre, served as director general of the Union Ltd.[79] For the Opera House, the first half of the 1920s was a period of permanent crisis: as a consequence of the hyperinflation of the time, singers and orchestral members struggled to make ends meet and went on strike several times. The directorate tried to remedy its financial problems through the acquisition of the Municipal Theatre, which became a second stage of the Opera House between 1921 and 1924.[80]

When examining the Budapest Offenbach performances of the interwar period, several new trends of contemporary operetta should be taken into account. The first of them is the Austro-Hungarian vogue of operettas about famous composers and their lives – in most cases romantic composers from the romanticized nineteenth century. (As far as I know, no operetta about Arnold Schoenberg, Igor Stravinsky, or Béla Bartók was written.)[81] Usually, the plots

---

[75] For the repertoire of the Folk Opera, see Klára Molnár, *A Népopera – Városi Színház, 1911–1951* [The folk opera – Municipal theatre, 1911–1951] (Budapest: OSZMI, 1998).

[76] 'A. B.' (probably August Beer), 'Volksoper', *Pester Lloyd* 59/212 (8 September 1912), 11.

[77] For an overview of interwar theatrical life, see Tamás Gajdó (ed.), *Magyar színháztörténet* [Hungarian theatre history], vol. 3: *1920–1949* (Budapest: Magyar Könyvklub, 2005).

[78] According to the original plans, the Union Ltd. was founded for the building of new theatres; these plans, however, failed to materialize.

[79] It should be noted that there were no familial ties between Jenő Rákosi and the later Communist dictator Mátyás Rákosi.

[80] For the contemporary repertoire of the Opera House, see Tibor Tallián's chapters in Géza Staud (ed.), *A budapesti Operaház 100 éve* [100 Years of the Budapest Opera House], 185–224.

[81] There was, however, *Der Zigeunerprimas* about the Rácz family of Gypsy musicians. See Micaela Baranello, *The Operetta Empire: Music Theatre in Early Twentieth-Century Vienna* (Oakland: University of California Press, 2021), 140–3.

of such pieces are quite schematic: the protagonist loves a woman, but his affection cannot be reciprocated; his love is unrequited or it is the composer himself who sacrifices it for the sake of his creativity. Instead of the traditional operetta happy ending with the union of the leading couple, most of the works end with the resignation of love, and the poor composer, alas, can find fulfilment only in creation. Hence, works of this kind typically belong to the subgenre of tragic operetta or *szomorú operett* (sad operetta), as Dezső Kosztolányi called it in one of his articles in 1921.[82]

The prototype and most succesful representative of the genre was Alfred Maria Willner and Heinz Reichert's *Das Dreimäderlhaus*, featuring Franz Schubert as the main protagonist, whose action set in Vienna in the 1820s. Although the music was compiled from Schubert's melodies by Heinrich Berté, the libretto handles the facts of the composer's life quite freely, all the more so because it was based on Schubert's novelized biography.[83] The world premiere took place during World War I, on 15 January 1916 in Wilhelm Karczag's Vienna Raimundtheater, but it was also premiered at the Budapest Gaiety Theatre in the same year on 23 April, in Zsolt Harsányi's translation as *Három a kislány* (*Das Dreimäderlhaus*, i. e., House of the Three Girls).[84] It was an immense success: following the 151st performance, the production was transferred to the more spacious Folk Opera/Municipal Theatre, where as early as October 1919 the 200th performance was celebrated. What is more, by 1925 it had premiered in every major operetta theatre of the capital: in the Buda Arena (15 June 1917) and at the Capital City Operetta Theatre (24 January 1922), as well as at the Király Theatre (23 August 1924). Its popularity is also attested by the parody entitled *Négy a kislány* (House of the Four Girls) by Géza Vágó, Emil Tábory, and Izsó Barna, which premiered at the Buda Arena on 11 August 1916. Beside its continuations, and its international success following World War I, several imitations of Berté's operetta were created by Budapest authors during the interwar period. To quote just two examples, István Bertha's *Chopin* was mounted at the Király Theatre on 4 December 1926, while the world premiere of Károly Komjáti's Liszt operetta, *Ein Liebestraum*, took place at the Theater an der Wien on 27 October 1934.

Another trend that had consequences for interwar Offenbach performances was the emergence of a new, younger generation of operetta composers during the 1920s, using more recent popular musical idioms, such as jazz, and new, fashionable dances like the foxtrot, shimmy, and Boston.

---

[82] Dezső Kosztolányi, 'Az új operett', [The New Operetta] *SzÉ* 10/6 (6–12 Feb. 1921), 1–2.

[83] Hans Rudolf Bartsch, *Schwammerl: Ein Schubert-Roman* (Leipzig: Staackmann, 1912).

[84] A manuscript copy of Harsányi's translation that was used as a stage manual of the Gaiety Theatre performances is kept in H-Bn, Theatre Department, Víg. 370.

Without doubt, the most internationally renowned representative of this trend in the Hungarian repertoire was Paul Ábrahám, whose *Viktória* (Victoria and Her Hussar) was premiered at the Budapest Király Theatre on 21 February 1930.[85] Nevertheless, many of his contemporaries – Dénes Buday, Mihály Krasznay-Krausz, Mihály Eisemann, Lajos Lajtai, Nicholas Brodszky, and Szabolcs Fényes – composed works in a similar style. What is more, even some older composers like Emmerich Kálmán adopted the new trends in their works. Meanwhile, old-fashioned operettas found their way into the Opera House.

From 1938, the discriminatory laws seriously affected both local Offenbach performances and theatrical life in general. Shortly after the adoption of the 'First Jewish Law', a Theatre and Film Arts Chamber was established, following the example of the Nazi *Reichstheaterkammer*. Everyone who worked at theatrical institutions (even opera singers, conductors, and orchestral musicians) was obliged to become a member, but the number of Jewish artists could not exceed the 20-per-cent ratio defined by the legislation. Subsequently, many people lost their livelihood as a result of racial discrimination.[86] In 1939, the unemployed artists organized a civil institution to aid each other: the OMIKE Artist's Action (az Országos Magyar Izraelita Kulturális Egyesület Művészakciója) gave closed performances in the Goldmark Hall and in two other small rooms.[87] The performances of the OMIKE Artist's Action continued until the German occupation in March 1944, when they were prohibited.[88]

---

[85] For the interwar repertoire of the Király Theatre, see Gyöngyi Heltai, 'A két háború közti pesti operett stiláris és ideológiai dilemmái: A Király Színház példája (1920–1936)' [Stylistic and ideological dilemmas of the interwar Budapest operetta: Through the example of the Király Theatre (1920–1936)]', *Tánctudományi Közlemények* 3/1 (2011), 53–68 (part 1); 3/2 (2011), 33–75 (part 2).

[86] Romsics, *A Horthy-korszak*, 343.

[87] The Goldmark Room is to be found in 7 Wesselényi Street (7th district, at the Dohány Street Great Synagogue). The two other rooms were situated at 21/b Hollán Street (5th district) and in 2 Bethlen Square (7th district).

[88] For the activity of Artist's Action, see Jenő Lévai (ed.), *Írók, színészek, énekesek és zenészek regényes életútja a Goldmark-teremig. Az OMIKE színháza és művészei* (Budapest: Faragó, 1943); in English: Jenő Lévai (ed.), *The Writers, Artists, Singers, and Musicians of the National Hungarian Jewish Cultural Association (OMIKE), 1939–1944*, expanded edition by Frederick Bondy, trans. by Anna Etawo (West Lafayette, IN: Purdue University Press, 2017). Further important general volumes concerning Artist's Action: László Harsányi, *A fényből a sötétbe: Az Országos Magyar Izraelita Közművelődési Egyesület, 1909–1950* [From light into darkness: The National Hungarian Jewish Cultural Association, 1909–1950] (Budapest: Napvilág Kiadó, 2019); Magda Horák, *Ősi hittel, becsülettel a hazáért! Országos Magyar Izraelita Közművelődési Egyesület, 1909–1944* [With ancient faith and honor for the homeland! The National Hungarian Jewish Cultural Association, 1909–1914] (Budapest: Háttér, 1998).

Offenbach as an Operetta Character

In June 1920, the following report appeared in the columns of the bourgeois radical daily newspaper *Világ*:

> The Municipal Theatre and the Király Theatre simultaneously plan to create operettas on some of the episodes of Offenbach's life, following the example of the Schubert operettas. The music will be arranged from Offenbach's own compositions. The Municipal Theatre has already commissioned Zsolt Harsányi and Frigyes Karinthy to write the libretto, while the Király Theatre invited Jenő Faragó to write the libretto, and Mihály Nádor to compile the music.[89]

As the text emphasizes, the similar plans of the two theatres were directly influenced by the local success of *Das Dreimäderlhaus*, and one of the librettists mentioned was the same Zsolt Harsányi who had translated Willner and Reichert's text into Hungarian. Only the Király Theatre's plan was realized: Faragó's piece, with Nádor's compilation from Offenbach's melodies, was premiered on 24 November 1920. There is no evidence that the other projected operetta was ever written and performed.

It reveals much about the taste of the contemporary Budapest public that this piece proved to be more popular at that time than the composer's own works. It was performed at the Király Theatre more than 200 times (the 200th performance was celebrated in October 1922).[90] It had an international impact, since it was also premiered at the Vienna Apollo-Theater (on 31 March 1922)[91] as well as the Prague Neues Deutsches Theater (on 18 October 1922)[92] in Robert Bodanzky and Bruno Hardt-Warden's German translation. According to Aladár Schöpflin, there was also a Munich premiere at the Theater am Gärtnerplatz on 28 August 1923, but this cannot be confirmed.[93] At the Berlin Komische Oper, it was adapted by James Klein and a certain Clarisson as *Der Meister von Montmartre* (premiere: 15 April 1922),[94] while the New York Century Theatre premiered Harry B. Smith's adaptation entitled *The Love Song*, with musical arrangement by Eduard Künneke (on 3 January 1925).[95]

---

[89] 'Két Offenbach-operette' [Two Offenbach Operettas], *Világ* 11/154 (29 June 1920), 3.

[90] Jenő Faragó, 'Offenbach 200', *Színházi Élet* 11/43 (22–28 October, 1922), 7.

[91] 'N. N.', 'Theater- und Kunstnachrichten', *Neue Freie Presse* no. 20685 (31 March 1922), 10 and L. Híd, 'Apollotheater', *Neue Freie Presse* no. 20687 (2 April 1922), 15.

[92] 'N. N.', 'Neues Deutsches Theater', *Prager Tagblatt* 47/244 (18 October 1922), 9 and R. M., 'Offenbach', *Prager Tagblatt* 47/246 (20 October 1922), 6.

[93] I would like to thank to Stefan Frey (Munich) for this information.

[94] 'N. N.', 'Komische Oper', *Vossische Zeitung* no. 178 (15 April 1922, morning edition), 4 and H. L. 'Komische Oper', *Vossische Zeitung* no. 180 (16 April 1922, morning edition), [3].

[95] Broadway Internet Database www.ibdb.com (accessed 1 June 2012).

In the context of contemporary operettas featuring composers, *Offenbach* is intriguing first of all because of the astonishing contradiction between the character of the titular hero and the way the subject is presented. Although the protagonist is the *buffo* musician of the nineteenth century par excellence, the operetta ends even more sadly than *Das Dreimäderlhaus*. What is more, the denouement is as tragic as possible: the work ends with a moving on-stage death scene in which Offenbach (played by Márton Rátkai, see Figure 2) breathes his last while the Barcarolle from his work in progress, *Les Contes d'Hoffmann*, is sung by his wife Herminie and a nurse. Finally, a doctor announces his death, in a manner similar to the final scene of Verdi's *La Traviata*.

Willner and Reichert's Schubert is not a handsome man and has only one beloved. By contrast, in Faragó's libretto, which is not without fictive elements, Offenbach is surrounded by a multitude of ladies. At the beginning of Act 1, he is playing blindman's buff with ten young girls. In Act 2, he is teaching the

Figure 2 Márton Rátkai as Offenbach and Erzsi Péchy as Empress Eugénie in Faragó and Nádor's *Offenbach* (photo by Angelo [Pál Funk], 1920)

ladies-in-waiting of Napoléon III's court how to dance the cancan – of course, to the music of the 'Galop infernal' from *Orphée aux enfers*. The source of the intrigue is that the composer has more love interests than necessary: Hortense Schneider (Juci Lábass), Herminie d'Alcaine (Marianne Abonyi), and the Empress Eugénie (Erzsi Péchy, see Figure 2), and he has a love affair with each of them. According to Faragó, the most tragic event is not Offenbach's death; the real tragedy of his life is that his ideal, Eugénie, remains unavailable to him until the end. Similarly to *Das Dreimäderlhaus*, the tragedy is the consequence of a misunderstanding. In Act 2, Hortense believes that Offenbach is having a liaison with the actress Mlle Theo, and she summons the court. In order to avoid a scandal, Herminie declares before the Emperor that it is she who loves the composer. She becomes his wife, and in Act 3, the exiled Empress can only send him a bouquet.

It should be noted that in the performances of Nádor and Faragó's operetta, even stage sets and costumes imitated Berté's Schubert operetta. In the stage manual of the Király Theatre – published by Sándor Marton as a lithographed manuscript[96] – several stage directions can be read according to which Eugénie and the female figurants wear Biedermeier clothes in Act 1, while in Act 3 Offenbach's work-room was furnished in Biedermeier style, although, in contrast to *Das Dreimäderlhaus*, this operetta is not set in the Vienna of the 1820s. Nádor's instrumentation is similar to that of Berté: his orchestra consists of two flutes, one piccolo, two oboes, two clarinets, two bassoons, four horns, two trumpets, three trombones, timpani, glockenspiel, celesta, triangle, a bass drum, a side drum, harp, and strings, while the protagonist also played the piano on the stage.[97] Berté used the same instruments plus tam-tam. It should be mentioned that the use of such instruments as harp, glockenspiel, and celesta is quite alien to Offenbach's own operettas.

The idea of an artist hero with three mistresses, and the episodic structure of the libretto come, however, not from *Das Dreimäderlhaus*, but from Offenbach's own posthumous opera, *Les Contes d'Hoffmann*. In the Budapest performance tradition of *Les Contes*, the central character usually had only three love interests, instead of four; this was either because of the deletion of the Antonia act, or because the framing acts were heavily abbreviated and Stella's role was cancelled (see Table 6). Faragó, who was an experienced journalist and playwright, used this constellation of characters in some of his other librettos, too. In *Casanova*, an operetta with Izsó Barna's music, premiered at the Folk Theatre on 11 October 1902, the hero of the title

---

[96] Music Collection fo the Hungarian Rádió, shelf mark: 15–41/B, pp. 4, 40, and 117.

[97] See Nádor's autograph full score: H-Bn, Music Department, Ms. mus. 10.930/1–3. As a conductor of the Király Theatre, Nádor used his own manuscript to perform the full score.

Table 6 The leading female roles in the Budapest performance history of *Les Contes d'Hoffmann*

Premiere	Olympia	Giulietta	Antonia	Stella
14 Apr. 1882 Folk Theatre	Aranka Hegyi	– [12/18 Jan 1882: Aranka Hegyi]	Aranka Hegyi	Aranka Hegyi
16 June 1890 Buda Arena	Mari Ligeti	–	Mari Ligeti	Mari Ligeti
15 Dec. 1900 Opera House	Bianca Bianchi	Bianca Bianchi	Bianca Bianchi	–
19 Jan. 1913 Opera House	Erzsi Sándor	Erzsi Sándor	Erzsi Sándor	Erzsi Sándor
24 May 1916 Buda Arena	Margit Kovács	–	Margit Kovács	Margit Kovács
28 March 1920 Opera House	Erzsi Sándor	Erzsi Sándor	Erzsi Sándor	–

conquers three women: Marion in Venice (Act 1), Madame Pompadour in Versailles (Act 2), and Lia in a Czech monastery, where he teaches the nuns to chant psalms (Act 3); the narrative frame consists of a prologue and an epilogue, where the main role is played by Satan himself (the equivalent of Lindorf, Coppélius, Dapertutto, and Miracle's role).[98] In *Chopin*, an operetta with István Bertha's music, premiered at the Király Theatre on 4 December 1926, the protagonist is in love with Józef Elsner's daughter Wanda, with George Sand, and the princess Eliza Radziwill; Act 1 ends with a spectacular grape-harvest festival, just as in the case of *Offenbach*.[99]

Besides *Les Contes d'Hoffmann* and *Das Dreimäderlhaus*, there was one more work, or rather theatrical production, which also influenced Nádor's operetta. Five months before the premiere of *Offenbach*, on 20 May 1920, *La Belle Hélène* was revived by the company of the Budapest Revue Theatre (Revü Színház) at one of the City Park's summer theatres, the Scala Theatre (Scala Színház), as *Szép Heléna*.[100] The libretto was newly translated by Imre Harmath and Frigyes Karinthy, a popular writer renowned first of all for his literary parodies.[101] According to contemporary press reports, the director of the company, István

---

[98] See the prompt book and stage manual of the Folk Theatre: H-Bn, Theatre Department, MM 5292.

[99] See a lithographed copy (Budapest: Sándor Marton, 1927) of the manuscript prompt book used at the Király Theatre: H-Bn, Theatre Department, MM 333.

[100] The orchestral parts used in this production are extant: H-Bn, Music Department, Népsz. 694/III–V.

[101] See Karinthy's autograph, used as prompt book for the performances of the Revü Theatre: H-Bn, Theatre Department, MM 16.286. The libretto was also published in the May–July 1920 issues of *Színházi Élet*.

Bródy, planned to invite Max Reinhardt to take the role of stage director, and Reinhardt's first *mise en scène* of the piece was premiered in the summer of 1911 at the Munich Künstlertheater, with Maria Jeritza in the title role and Alexander von Zemlinsky as conductor. In the end, the import of the Munich production was cancelled, and the Revue Theatre production was directed by Bródy himself, who had earlier worked as a stage manager at the Budapest Hungarian Theatre (1905–6) and Opera House (1913–18), as well as at the Vienna Carl-Theater (1912). Erzsi Péchy in the title role proved to be particularly successful, which was the reason why she was chosen for the role of Eugénie in Nádor and Faragó's *Offenbach*. In the work performed at the Király Theatre, there are several allusions to *La Belle Hélène*. Hortense repeatedly asks the question: who will sing the role of the Fair Helen? Her question is answered in Act 3, when the death-sick Offenbach has a vision. At first, Hortense appears as the Grand Duchess of Gerolstein, then Eugénie appears as Helen, singing the couplets 'Amours divins …' from Offenbach's *opéra bouffe*. All in all, *Offenbach* drew on both Austro-Hungarian tradition and the protagonist's own works.

One more allusion in Faragó's libretto also deserves attention. In Act 2, at the beginning of the finale, when Offenbach confesses his love to Eugénie, he quotes a poem from Heinrich Heine's *Buch der Lieder* in Hungarian translation:

> OFFENBACH:
> Tedd szívemre kicsi kezedet, édes;
> Hallod, milyen lárma és ketyegés ez?
> Egy gonosz ács dolgozik most odabenn,
> Jaj, a koporsómat ácsolja nekem!
>
> Ácsol, zakatol, napokon, éjjen át,
> Pihenni nem enged, aludni se hágy!
> Végezd be, te zordon ács már szaporán,
> Hadd aludjam végképp azután!
> *(Nádor and Faragó:* Offenbach, *Act 2, Scene 14)*[102]

> *Lieb Liebchen, leg's Händchen aufs Herze mein; –*
> *Ach, hörst du, wie's pochet im Kämmerlein,*
> *Da hauset ein Zimmermann schlimm und arg,*
> *Der Zimmert mir einen Totensarg.*
>
> *Es hämmert und klopfet bei Tag und bei Nacht;*
> *Es hat mich schon längst um den Schlaf gebracht.*
> *Ach! sputet Euch, Meister Zimmermann,*
> *Damit ich balde schlafen kann.*
> *(Heine:* Buch der Lieder, Junge Leiden / Lieder, *no. 4)*

---

[102] H-Bn, MM 16.562, p. 89.

(Love, my love, – lay your small hand on my heart,
Hear, every second, a beat and a start!
There dwells a carpenter, – evil is he, –
Always at work on a coffin for me.

He hammers by night, and he hammers by day;
Long he has driven my sleep far away;
Hammer, old carpenter, hammer your best!
So that I quickly may go to my rest.

Translated by Charles G. Leland)

It should be noted that the Heine quotation has no trace in Bodanzky and Hardt-Warden's translation. The corresponding passage in the Vienna version is as follows:

OFFENBACH:
O rosenrote Stunde,
Wo verlangend das Herz zum Herzen sich neigt!
Will küssen deinen Mund,
Der sprechen will und schweigt![103]

(O rose-red time,
when a heart leans longing to the other!
I want to kiss your mouth,
which wants to speak but remains silent.)

The contemporary Budapest press evaluated the production according to their prejudices.[104] It is not surprising that the anonymous critic of the conservative daily newspaper *Budapesti Hírlap* wrote a panegyric on the operetta, emphasizing: 'the plot of the piece is lively and animated, [and] it is full of effective points',[105] since both the Király Theatre and the newspaper in question were the property of the Rákosi-Beöthy family. The theatre belonged to the Union Ltd., led by László Beöthy, while the editor-in-chief of *Budapesti Hírlap* was his uncle, Jenő Rákosi. Even the tabloids *Színház és Divat* and *8 Órai Újság* overpraised Nádor and Faragó's piece, finding that '*Offenbach* [was] one of the most sensational operettas of the past years',[106] and that 'the task of interpreting Offenbach's lovely melodies and the witty libretto, free of

---

[103] H-Bn, Theatre Department, IM 1146, p. 35.

[104] On the Budapest press of the period, see Balázs Sipos, *Sajtó és hatalom a Horthy-korszakban* [Press and power in the Horthy era] (Budapest: Argumentum Kiadó, 2011) and Erika N. Mandl, *Színház a magyar sajtóban a két világháború között* [Theatre in the Hungarian press in the interwar period] (Budapest: Argumentum Kiadó, 2012).

[105] 'N. N.', '*Offenbach*: A Király Színház bemutatója' [*Offenbach*: Premiere of the Király Theatre], *Budapesti Hírlap* 40/278 (25 November 1920), 5.

[106] 'F. p.' [Pál Forró], '*Offenbach*', *Színház és Divat* 5/43 (4 December 1920), 7–8.

conventional operetta exaggerations, was solved with full success by the actors'.[107] *Színház és Divat* was founded by Faragó himself in 1916, who edited it until 1918. From 1919 until 1930 – that is, even at the time of the premiere – he was the managing editor of *8 Órai Újság*.

By contrast, it is rather surprising what an unusually moderate and favourable review of the production appeared in *Új Nemzedék*, one of the otherwise not-too-sophisticated far-right press organs. According to the anonymous critic: 'Jenő Faragó exploits his idea, which gives us a chance to hear Offenbach's finest melodies in due measure and with style.' The critic found that Nádor was 'himself an outstanding artist, and the music numbers operate[d] in his hands with the ecstasy of French champagne'. The same author also stated: 'Offenbach, the son of a Cologne rabbi, remains captivating and timely beyond all trends'.[108] Edited by István Milotay, *Új Nemzedék* was the organ of the antisemitic race-protectionist movement.[109] Although Milotay left the editorial board some time before the premiere of *Offenbach*, the journal belonged to the Central Press Corporation, a media trust founded by the Jesuit monk Béla Bangha, the 'press apostle' of 'Christian-National' propaganda.[110] Somewhat more typical of this political direction is the anonymous review published in *Nemzeti Újság*, another far-right organ of the Central Press Corporation, which particularly criticized the libretto and the actor playing the title role. According to the author of the article, '*Das Dreimäderlhaus* was as successful as the present attempt is unlucky, in which the role of Offenbach is handed off to a voiceless comedian, the otherwise nice and gifted Rátkai.'[111]

The heaviest criticism, however, appeared not in the far-right press, but in a music magazine. The article, signed by 'n.' in *Zenei Hét*, whose editor was the otherwise quite unknown Béla Kornél Melléky, expressed his antipathy in the following way:

> Jacques Offenbach was a very good composer and wrote many fine operettas. Why are they not performed? Meilhac and Halévy were the wittiest librettists of the operatic literature of their time. It seems that they were not good enough for the Király Theatre. The task of the librettist of the present operetta was all the more difficult because he had to make his hero deliver a plethora of the wittiest bon mots, since Offenbach was one of the wittiest people in the Paris of his time. But for the Király Theatre, neither Offenbach's own music

---

[107] 'N. N.', 'Az *Offenbach* premierje' [The premiere of *Offenbach*], *8 Órai Újság* 6/279 (26 November 1920), 5.

[108] 'N. N.', '*Offenbach*', *Új Nemzedék* 2/281 (28 November 1920), 6.

[109] Gyurgyák, *Magyar fajvédők*, 169–84 and 257–8. [110] Ibid., 73–86 and 243–4.

[111] 'N. N.', '*Offenbach* (Operettbemutató a Király Színházban)' [*Offenbach*: An operetta premiere at the Király Theatre], *Nemzeti Újság* 11/276 (25 November 1920), 4.

nor Meilhac's witty libretto were good enough. There was need for a much weaker librettist and a music tailor who dissects it in order to make from all these a completely new thing, which contains a little bit from everything, and which, when put together – is nothing.[112]

In light of this review, it will be instructive to compare this production and its press response with another case, in which Offenbach's own music was performed in the most prestigious institution of Budapest's theatrical life.

The Brigands Seize Power

The Opera House was attacked by armed bandits, director Radnai was sought high and low, fortunately, however, he was not found. . . . Yesterday, the latent discontent broke into overt revolt. Some of the membership founded a gang of robbers and, under the pretence of performing an operetta, they seized power over the Opera House.[113]

Needless to say, the text quoted is a joke: the satirical magazine *Az Ojság* responded with these words to the fact that Offenbach's *A banditák* (*Les Brigands*) was programmed to be performed at the Opera House on All Fool's Day 1933. Operetta performances had had a certain tradition there even before then. Offenbach's *Le Mariage aux lanternes* had been performed at the Opera during Mahler's directorship in 1890, and soon after other 'classical' operettas had been programmed: Johann Strauss, Jr's *Die Fledermaus* (for the first time on 10 May 1895) and *Die Zigeunerbaron* (first performed there on 27 May 1905). Between 1921 and 1924, when the Municipal Theatre functioned as a second stage of the Opera House, the two theatres had a shared company, and opera singers regularly participated in the operetta performances on both stages. For example, *Orphée aux enfers* was successfully revived at the Municipal Theatre on 22 September 1923 as *Orpheus a pokolban*, with the 'warm-toned' József Gábor in the title role.[114] Gábor, who debuted at the Opera House as Nicklausse in *Les Contes d'Hoffmann* on 15 December 1900, sang there until 1908, and again from 1913 until his death in 1929. He took important operatic roles, such as Herod in Richard Strauss's *Salome* (premiered on 19 December 1912) or Pelléas in Debussy's *Pelléas et Mélisande* (premiered on 29 November 1925). He even worked as stage director of the Opera House during the 1926/27 season.[115]

---

[112] 'N.', '*Offenbach*', *Zenei Hét* 1/11 (28 November 1920), 8–9.

[113] 'N. N.', 'Zsákbanditák az Operában' [Sack bandits in the Opera House], *Az Ojság* 14/15 (9 April 1933), 5. 'Zsákbanditák' is an untranslatable wordplay, including Offenbach's first name, Jacques, phonetically transcribed as 'zsák', which means 'sack' in Hungarian.

[114] 'N. N.', 'Orpheus az alvilágban' [Orpheus in the underworld], *Budapesti Hírlap* 43/214 (23 September 1923), 10.

[115] For Gábor's career, see György Székely (ed.), *Magyar színházművészeti lexikon* [Hungarian lexicon for theatre arts] (Budapest: Akadémiai Kiadó, 1994), 241.

However, operetta performances at the Opera House became more frequent in the second half of Miklós Radnai's directorship (1925–35) following the Great Depression, so much so that between 1930 and 1935 one operetta was premiered in each season, a phenomenon which can be attributed first of all to financial concerns. Nevertheless, the stylistic changes in popular stage music mentioned in Section 2 likewise played a role. The works chosen were either nineteenth-century pieces like *Rip van Winkle* by Planquette (6 December 1935) and *Der Zigeunerbaron* (1 May 1932), or more recent operettas by native composers, such as Lehár's *Das Land des Lächelns* (20 December 1930) and *Guiditta* (8 April 1934). In both cases, the music stands significantly closer to nineteenth-century operatic style than did contemporary jazz operettas.

As stated in the reviews that followed the Budapest premiere, the idea of reviving Offenbach's *Les Brigands* came from Berlin,[116] where the Charlottenburg Städtische Oper staged the piece on 29 May 1932 in Gustaf Gründgens's adaptation[117] with such great success that the same production was taken to Leipzig and Hamburg.[118] Furthermore, the work had been staged at the Paris Opéra-Comique in 1931, so perhaps the Berlin and Budapest productions thus reflected the newfound canonic status conferred on this work by its acceptance into the Opéra-Comique repertoire. Although some Hungarian critics, for example Margit Prahács, reviewer of the conservative monthly literary magazine *Napkelet*, claimed that this operetta by Offenbach was completely unknown previously in the capital,[119] this claim needs to be corrected. In fact, *Les Brigands* was premiered in Budapest as early as 5 July 1870 at the Wollgasse German Theatre as *Die Banditen*.[120] One year after the German premiere, Endre Latabár's troupe also staged the work on 25 June 1871 in his Hungarian translation, entitled *A rablók*,[121] which was frequently performed during the 1880s and 1890s by Ignác Krecsányi's itinerant troupe, whose most important places of activity were Pressburg,

---

[116] Ervin Ybl, '*A banditák*. Offenbach vígoperájának bemutatója' [*Les Brigands*: The premiere of Offenbach's comic opera], *Budapesti Hírlap* 53/75 (2 April 1933), 15.

[117] 'N. N.' [Theatre programme], *Vossische Zeitung* no. 257 (29 May 1932, morning edition), [16]; Edwin Neruda, '*Die Banditen*: Städtische Oper', *Vossische Zeitung* no. 258 (30 May 1932, evening edition), [9].

[118] Stephan Stompor, 'Die Offenbach-Renaissance um 1930 und die geschlossenen Vorstellungen für Juden nach 1933', in Franke (ed.), *Offenbach und die Schauplätze*, 257–8.

[119] Margit Prahács, 'Zene' [Music], *Napkelet* 11/5 (1 May 1933), 390–1.

[120] *Deutscher Bühnen-Almanach*, vol. 35, ed. by A. Entsch (Berlin: n.p., 1871), 242. The song texts were even published in print: H-Bn, Central Collection, 203.599: *Die Banditen. Operette in 3 Akten von Meilhac und Halévy. Deutsch von Richard Genée. Musik von Jacques Offenbach* (Pest: Alois Bucsánszky, 1870).

[121] 'N. N.', 'Irodalom, színház, művészet' [Literature, theatre, art], *Hon* 9/145 (26 June 1871), [2].

Timişoara, and Buda.[122] One thing is certain, however: performing *Les Brigands* at the Opera House was definitely a new idea. Since the 1890 premiere of *Eljegyzés lámpafénynél*, Offenbach's only work programmed there had been *Les Contes d'Hoffmann*.

It is all the more instructive to compare the press response to these two productions. In 1890, when *Les Contes* still belonged to the repertoire of popular theatres, Mahler's decision to programme Offenbach at the Opera House was highly debated. In 1933, however, there was no critic who questioned the propriety of presenting Offenbach's music at the same institution. Bafflingly enough, even 'M. I.', the author of the review published in the far-right daily newspaper *Magyarság*, found that 'Offenbach is an excellent, reputed old firm, a wholesale melody dealer, with its own original mine of melodies.'[123] This is all the more surprising since, in all likelihood, 'M. I.' was István Milotay, who as already mentioned was a notable figure of the race-protectionist movement and editor-in-chief of the journal, who later, as a deputy of the Hungarian Parliament, supported the anti-Jewish laws.[124] Even if it is possible to read this review as tinged with a bit of antisemitism (Offenbach's music is *commercial*, i.e., created 'wholesale', rather than for some spiritual ideal), it is considerably milder than one would expect.

It should be noted that to ensure success, the Opera House deployed its best forces. Falsacappa was played by Ferenc Székelyhidy (see Figure 3), an excellent tenor, who regularly sang such roles as Walther von Stolzing in Wagner's *Die Meistersinger von Nürnberg*, Canio in Leoncavallo's *Pagliacci*, or Don Ottavio in Mozart's *Don Giovanni*.[125] This was not his first Offenbach role: in 1920 it was he who had sung Paris in the reprise of *La Belle Hélène*. The brigand chief's daughter, Fiorella, was Lujza Szabó, a young coloratura soprano, 'whose pleasant character [and] excellent vocal culture also prevailed in this role',[126] although she mostly represented such serious stage heroines as the Queen of the Night in Mozart's *Die Zauberflöte*, or Gilda in Verdi's *Rigoletto*.[127] The role of Fiorella's inamorato, Fragoletto – originally a trouser role created by Zulma Bouffar – was given to the young tenor Endre Rösler,[128] who excelled first of all in roles such as Belmonte in Mozart's *Die Entführung aus dem Serail* and Fernando in *Così fan tutte*.

---

[122] See the manuscript prompt book from Krecsányi's estate (H-Bn, Theatre Department, MM 13.884). A manuscript stage manual likewise from Krecsányi's estate and dated 19 June 1889 (H-Bn, Theatre Department, MM 6935) contains another Hungarian translation by István Toldy.

[123] 'M. I. ', 'Offenbach-bemutató az Operaházban. *A banditák* premierje' [Offenbach Premiere at the Opera House. The First Performance of *Les Brigands*], *Magyarság* 14/75 (2 April 1933), 17.

[124] Gyurgyák, *A zsidókérdés*, 140 and 444–445.

[125] Székely (ed.), *Magyar színházművészeti lexikon*, 734.

[126] Ybl, '*A banditák*', *Budapesti Hírlap* 53/75 (2 April 1933), 15.

[127] Székely (ed.), *Magyar színházművészeti lexikon*, 715.   [128] Ibid., 660.

Figure 3 Ferenc Székelyhidy as Falsacappa with his female bandits in
A banditák (photo by Pál Varga M.)

The eventful *mise en scène* was directed by László Márkus, at that time head of
the National Theatre.[129] His 'inimitable scenic genius'[130] was widely acknowledged. Gusztáv Oláh's set scenes and costumes and Antal Fleischer's conducting
were likewise acknowledged, along with Zsolt Harsányi's Hungarian translation.
Unfortunately, it is impossible to investigate whether Harsányi's text was as rich
in topical allusions as Gründgens's adaptation, since no copy of the full libretto of

---

[129] Ibid., 489.
[130] 'N. N.', 'Két bemutató a M. Kir. Operaházban' [Two premieres at the Roy. Hun. Opera House],
A Zene 14/16 (1 May 1933), 306–7.

the production survives.[131] The only element of the production which divided opinions was Jan Cieplinski's ballet choreography, heavily criticized by, among others, Sándor Jemnitz, a composer and Schoenberg disciple, and critic for the social democrat daily newspaper *Népszava*.[132]

All in all, mounting *Les Brigands* on the stage of the Budapest Opera House proved to be a definite success.

Offenbach in Exile

The 1933 production of *A banditák* demonstrates that even in the middle of the Horthy era, it was possible to perform one of the composer's *opéras bouffes* on the most prestigious stage of the capital. However, by the end of the 1930s the situation had changed radically.

As already mentioned, in 1939, following the passage of the first anti-Jewish law, a civil cultural institution named OMIKE Artist's Action was founded. The OMIKE (National Hungarian Jewish Cultural Association) itself was not new and originally it did not serve charitable aims. Although it aided indigent people during World War I[133] and supported those Jewish students who were forced to study abroad following the *numerus clausus* law,[134] it was originally founded in 1909 for the promotion of religious thinking.[135] Artist's Action, however, came into existence expressly to support those performing artists who had lost their livelihood as a consequence of the anti-Jewish laws. The key figure in organizing OMIKE was Géza Ribáry, an attorney and vice-president of the Israelite Congregation of Pest, but several artists likewise played an important role – among others Lajos Bálint, head of the dramatic company, who earlier worked as the dramaturge of the Budapest National Theatre,[136] and the stage manager László Bánóczi – both were members of the avant-gardist Thalia Society (1904–8).[137] Although OMIKE's activities were permitted by the authorities,[138] circulation of their playbills was prohibited,[139] and the pieces performed had to be first submitted for approval to the censors.[140] All in all, Artist's Action and the character of its performances were quite similar to those of the corresponding Berlin institution called the Jüdischer Kulturbund.[141] According to the organization's own statistics, in the 1939/40 season, 40,000 spectators attended its performances; during the next season, this figure

---

[131] Most of the performing materials are lost; only the manuscript copies of some roles without music are extant: H-Bn, Music Department, ZBK 201/h.

[132] Sándor Jemnitz, '*A banditák*: Offenbach-siker az Operaházban' [*Les Brigands*: An Offenbach success at the Opera House], *Népszava* 61/76 (2 April 1933), 8.

[133] Horák, *Ősi hittel,* 100–3, 111–13, 119–21 and 126–7.   [134] Ibid., 173.   [135] Ibid., 23.

[136] Székely (ed.), *Magyar színházművészeti lexikon*, 48.   [137] Ibid., 57.

[138] Lévai, *Írók, színészek,* 64.   [139] Ibid., 21.   [140] Ibid., 20.

[141] See Stompor, 'Die Offenbach-Renaissance', 257–66.

increased to 60,000, while in the 1941/42 and 1942/43 seasons, the number of spectators were 80,000 and 92,000, respectively.[142]

The closed performances – as the extant programme booklets of the events attest[143] – comprised diverse genres: classical orchestral concerts, chamber music evenings, jazz matinées, cabarets, performances of oratorios, operas, spoken plays, and operettas. Musicological writings investigating the repertoire of this dark period usually focus – understandably – on the 'serious' repertoire. Tibor Tallián has dedicated important studies to the operatic repertoire[144] and premieres by contemporary composers,[145] while János Mácsai has published an article on classical music performances in general.[146] In accordance with the subject of this study, I deal here only with the Offenbach repertoire. It should be noted that the press reports documenting Artist's Action's activities are significantly scantier than reports on theatres working under normal circumstances since discrimination seriously affected the press, too, and by the end of the 1930s some important and long-established newspapers had ceased to exist.

All three stages were quite small. The most spacious one, in the Goldmark Room, could accommodate only 382 spectators. The width of its stage was just 7 metres, its usable depth 6.3 metres, and its proscenium was 4 metres high by 5 metres wide. Furthermore, there was no separate orchestral pit.[147] For such a tiny stage, Offenbach's one-acters might have been an ideal choice. Hence, it is not surprising that already in the first season, on 11 February 1940, *Un Mari à la porte* was staged as *A férj kopogtat* with István Zádor's historicizing stage sets. According to the *Magyar Zsidók Lapja*'s press report, it was played 'with pretty great success', and 'the audience of the jam-packed room expressed its satisfaction with unending applause'.[148] This was followed in the next season by the premiere of *Le Mariage aux lanternes* in Sándor Fischer's new translation as *Eljegyzés lámpafénynél*. According to a press report, Fischer, a composer and

[142] H-Bn, Theatre Department, Irattár 152, fol. 3. Typewritten circular to the members of Artist's Action.

[143] H-Bn, Theatre Department, OMIKE. Most of the documents kept under this shelf mark are also available online on the homepage www.omike.hu, edited by László Harsányi.

[144] Tibor Tallián, 'Az OMIKE Művészakció operaszínpada, 1940–1944' [The operatic stage of the OMIKE Artist's Action, 1940–1944], *Muzsika* 39/1 (January 1996), 14–18.

[145] Tibor Tallián, 'Magyar zsidó szerzők bemutatói, 1940–1944' [Premieres of Hungarian Jewish composers], in Tibor Tallián, *Magyar képek: Fejezetek a magyar zeneélet és zeneszerzés történetéből, 1940–1956* [Hungarian pictures: Chapters of the history of Hungarian musical life and composition, 1940–1956] (Budapest: Balassi/MTA BTK, 2014), 75–80.

[146] János Mácsai, 'Az OMIKE zenei előadásai, 1939–1944' [The musical performances of OMIKE, 1939–1944], *Magyar Zene* 52/4 (November 2014), 441–51.

[147] Lévai, *Írók, színészek*, 19. Unfortunately, we do not have the dimensions of the smaller commercial theaters during the interwar period.

[148] 'N. N.', 'Az OMIKE előadásai', *Magyar Zsidók Lapja* 2/7 (15 February 1940), 5. Most of the journal's issues are available in the digital collection of the Tel Aviv National Library: http://web.nli.org.il/sites/JPress/English/Pages/default.aspx (accessed 18 May 2017).

theatre conductor who had studied at the Budapest Liszt Academy of Music,[149] accompanied the performance on the piano.[150] According to the evidence of some preliminary programme plans, in the 1940/41 and 1941/42 seasons the premieres of two more Offenbach one-acters, *A Kofák* [*Mesdames de la Halle*] and *A varázshegedű* [*Le Violoneux*] were also planned.[151] In the absence of press reports, however, it is quite likely that these performances did not take place; the same is true for the only full-evening *opéra bouffe*, *Kékszakáll* (*Barbe-bleue*), which was planned to be performed in full during the 1942/43 season.[152] It is doubtful whether the Offenbach revue compiled by Ferenc Bermann, whose premiere is dated in the programme booklet to 10 November 1942, took place. According to the booklet, it comprised music numbers from *Orphée aux enfers*, *La Belle Hélène*, *La Grande-Duchesse de Gérolstein*, *Le Mariage aux lanternes*, *La Vie Parisienne*, and *Les Contes d'Hoffmann*.[153]

If the programming of one-act operettas was a logical consequence of the size of the stage, the same cannot be said about the performances of *Les Contes d'Hoffmann*. The posthumous opera was premiered in the Goldmark Room on 13 January 1941 in a concert performance, but with the assistance of an orchestra comprising forty instrumentalists and a choir consisting of twenty-four singers.[154] This ensemble was organized by the conductor Vilmos Komor, who had earlier played the violin in the orchestra of the Opera House and conducted at the Budapest Municipal Theatre as well as at several other theatres.[155] On 9 November 1942, Offenbach's opera was even presented in a new production under Komor's baton, a fully staged performance directed by Ernő Szabolcs, 'who made a real miracle on the small stage'.[156] The press report also highlighted the stage sets, made by István Zádor: they were found so beautiful that the scenery of the Antonia act was applauded by the audience.[157] This episode was played as Act 3, following the Venetian tableau; the cast of characters also reveals that the framing acts were shortened, since Stella's name is missing (see Figure 4).

---

[149] For his biography, see Aladár Schöpflin, *Magyar színművészeti lexikon* [Hungarian lexicon of theater arts], vol. 2 (Budapest: Országos Színészegyesület és Nyugdíjintézete, 1929–31), 43. and 'N. N.', 'Búcsúzunk. Fischer Sándor' [Obituary: Sándor Fischer], *Muzsika* 38/4 (April 1995), 45.

[150] 'N. N.', 'Az OMIKE Művészakció' [OMIKE Artist's Action], *Magyar Zsidók Lapja* 3/8 (20 February 1941), 6.

[151] H-Bn, Theatrical Department, OMIKE.   [152] Ibid.   [153] Ibid.

[154] Ibid. An undated typewritten list of the musicians contains, however, many more names; it is quite likely that the eighty-three instrumentalists and thirty-seven choir singers mentioned in this document never played together.

[155] For his biography, see Ágnes Komor, *Apám, Komor Vilmos* [My father, Vilmos Komor] (Budapest: Táltos GM, 1986).

[156] 'N. N.', 'Hoffmann meséi' [The tales of Hoffmann], *Magyar Zsidók Lapja* 4/46 (12 November 1942), 12.

[157] Ibid.

OMIKE MŰVÉSZAKCIÓ

——————— A GOLDMARK-TEREMBEN ———————

Nov, 9-én, hétfőn este 6 órakor (**1.**-ször) Helybizt.: **O/2, Z/1**
Nov, 16-án, hétfőn este 6 órakor (**2.**-szor) Helybizt.: **O/3**
Nov. 18-án, szerdán este 6 órakor (**3.**-szor) Helybizt.: **O/1, Z/2**

> Operai szelvénytöbblet fizetendő!

Offenbach

Hoffmann meséi

Dalmű 3 felvonásban (4 képben)

Személyek:

	nov. 9-én és 16-án	nov. 18-án
Olympia … … … … …	*Darvas Ibolya*	*Ladányi Ilona*
Giulietta … … … … …⎫		*Gödry Kató*
Antonia … … … … …⎭	*Relle Gabriella*	*Pogány Zsuzsi*
Lindorf … … … … …⎫		
Coppelius … … … …⎧	*Farkas Sándor*	*Lendvay Andor*
Dapertutto … … …⎩		
Mirakel … … … … …		
Hoffmann … … … …	*Fehér Pál*	*Teszler Tivadar*
Miklós … … … … …	*Spiegel Annie*	*Somogyi Piri*
András … … … …⎫		
Pitichinaccio … …⎬	*Teszler Tivadar*	*Rózsa Nándor*
Cochenille … … …⎭		
Anya hangja … … …	*Sik Olga*	*Spiegel Annie*
Spalanzani … … …	*Somogyi Dezső*	*Somogyi Dezső*
Nathaniel … … … …	*Ney Dávid*	*Ney Dávid*
Crespel … … … … …	*Bálint Béla*	*Bálint Béla*
Luther … … … … …	*Molnár László*	*Molnár László*
Hermann … … … …	*Galsay Ervin*	*Galsay Ervin*
Schlemil… … … … …	*Roth Ferenc*	*Roth Ferenc*

Vezényel **Komor Vilmos**　　　Rendező **Szabolcs Ernő**

Karigazgató **dr. Bermann Ferenc**

Színpadi előadás　　　　Az Omike zene- és énekkara

Kezdete pontosan 6 órakor

8

Figure 4 Playbill of the first three closed performances of *Les Contes d'Hoffmann* at the Goldmark Hall in November 1942 Reproduced by kind permission of the Theatre History Collection of the National Széchényi Library Budapest

Even a cursory look at the leading roles shows that excellent singers contributed to the Offenbach performances. Olympia's role was sung by coloratura soprano Ilona Ladányi, who played Fanchette in *Le Mariage aux lanternes* and was a member of the Budapest Opera House between 1932 and 1939, and again from 1945 to 1949. In Artist's Action's productions, she performed such roles as

Astaroth in *Die Königin von Saba*,[158] Konstanze in *Die Entführung aus dem Serail*,[159] and Gilda in *Rigoletto*.[160] Gabriella Relle, the Giulietta and Antonia of *Les Contes d'Hoffmann*, likewise lost her Opera House job. She had debuted there in 1924 as Elsa in *Lohengrin*,[161] and had sung the leading roles of Wagner and Puccini operas; perhaps her most memorable role was Liù in *Turandot*.[162] Pál Fehér, who sang the title role of *Les Contes d'Hoffmann* and Pierre in *Le Mariage aux lanternes*, performed from 1927 at the Berlin Kroll-Oper and Städtische Oper, and not only created Napoléon in the first performance of Emmerich Kálmán's *Kaiserin Joséphine* in Zurich but also the Painter in the world premiere of Alban Berg's *Lulu*.[163] The baritone Sándor Farkas, singing the triple role of Coppélius, Dapertutto, and Miracle, debuted at the Budapest Opera House in 1917 as Tonio in *Pagliacci*.[164] He created Michele in the local premiere of *Il tabarro*,[165] but he also sang Don Fernando in *Fidelio*.[166]

Following World War II, the revival of *Les Contes d'Hoffmann* at the Budapest Opera House on 1 March 1946 under Vilmos Komor's baton marked the occasion of Offenbach's return from exile, and much more besides. As conductor György Lehel, the critic of the daily newspaper *Haladás* wrote,

> [i]t is obvious that the Association of New Opera Friends intended the revival of *Les Contes d'Hoffmann*, put on the index seven years before, much more as a political demonstration and a theatrical delicacy than as a musical event. They wanted to symbolize through this performance the liberty of art and thought.[167]

4 Offenbach during the Rákosi Era, 1949–1956

Historical Context

At the end of World War II, Hungary was occupied by Soviet troops – the capital city was taken by Russian soldiers on 13 February 1945, following a bloody siege during which many civilians were killed and Budapest was razed. On the one hand, the Soviet invasion meant the liberation of the populace from German

---

[158] *Magyar Zsidók Lapja* 4/9 (26 February 1942), 6.

[159] *Magyar Zsidók Lapja* 3/5 (30 January 1940), 6.

[160] *Magyar Zsidók Lapja* 3/10 (6 March 1940), 6.   [161] *Pesti Napló* 75/111 (7 June 1924), 7.

[162] *Zenei Szemle* 12/1–2 (January–February 1928), 30–2.

[163] László Markó (ed.), *Új magyar életrajzi lexikon* [New Hungarian biographical lexicon], vol. 2 (Budapest: Magyar Könyvklub/Helikon Kiadó, 2001), 560; *Großes Sängerlexikon*, ed. by K. J. Kutsch and Leo Riemens (Munich: Saur, 2003), vol. 2, 1418.

[164] *Budapesti Hírlap* 37/259 (19 October 1917), 7.

[165] *Pesti Napló* 73/281 (10 December 1922), 3.

[166] *Magyar Zsidók Lapja* 4/14 (1 April 1942), 6.

[167] György Lehel, 'A *Hoffmann meséi* felújítása' [The revival of *Les Contes d'Hoffmann*], *Haladás* 2/9 (14 March 1946), 4.

occupation, while at the same time it also meant new tribulations for many: the mass rape of women and forced labour in the Soviet Union. The long-term consequence was that the country became part of the Soviet sphere of interest and adopted its political system.[168]

At the beginning, however, invaders and local Communists exercised tactical self-control. So much so that the anti-fascist Provisional National Government, formed as a multiparty coalition government on 22 December 1944 in Debrecen, was led by Miklós Béla Dálnoki, a military officer who had deserted Horthy's army. Its first measures were the declaration of an armistice with the Allies and the impeachment of war criminals. Despite the seeming parliamentarism, however, in the short 'Coalition Period' (1945–7), the Allied Control Commission, headed by Marshal Kliment Voroshilov and the Hungarian Communist Party, exerted decisive influence on the course of events, although on the occasion of the 1945 general elections, Communists earned only 17 per cent of the vote. The majority of the populace (57 per cent) voted for the Smallholders' Party, despite the fact that Communists sought to make political capital of the most popular measure for the provisional government: the radical agrarian reform that redistributed the lands that had previously been privately owned and middle-sized estates. Although Smallholders and social democrats might have been able to form a two-party government, under Voroshilov's pressure, even the Communist Party got three portfolios in Zoltán Tildy's new government, including the politically important Ministry of Interior. Hence, despite the fact that on 31 January 1946 Hungary was declared a democratic republic, it is better to call the few years of transition following World War II the age of 'pre-Stalinization'.[169]

Under such circumstances, the first few years following World War II were relatively uneventful from the point of view of Offenbach's reception: the only production worth mentioning is a reprise of *Szép Heléna* (*La Belle Hélène*) at the Capital City Operetta Theatre on 10 April 1948, with operatic soprano Eszter Réthy in the title role and popular comic actor Kálmán Latabár as Menelaos. As a matter of fact, István Zágon's Hungarian translation was based not on Meilhac and Halévy's libretto, but on Egon Friedell and Hans Sassmann's adaptation, the music for which was arranged by Erich Wolfgang Korngold.[170] In the case of this theatrical reprise, only the jokes alluding to the

---

[168] Romsics, *Magyarország története*, 270–384.

[169] György Gyarmati, *A Rákosi-korszak* [The Rákosi era] (Budapest: ÁBTL–Rubicon, 2013), 28–111.

[170] Staged by Max Reinhardt, this adaptation was premiered on 15 June 1931 at the Berlin Theater am Kurfürstendamm. See Edwin Neruda, 'Reinhardt's *Schöne Helena*', *Vossische Zeitung* no. 279 (16 June 1931, evening edition), 3.

political reality of the one-time Horthy era and the red stars decorating the theatre playbill signalled that a new period had begun.

The real aims of the Soviet Union and the Communists towards Hungary began to become clear at the beginning of 1947. On 25 February of that year, Béla Kovács, the secretary of the government party and a member of the Hungarian Parliament, was arrested and deported to the Soviet Union by the Soviet military authorities, violating his diplomatic immunity. In March, a significant change occurred in international politics when US President Truman declared the containment of Soviet geopolitical expansion as the main goal of American foreign policy. This act meant the beginning of the Cold War and resulted in a change of policy in Hungary. On 20 May 1947, prime minister Ferenc Nagy was forced to resign by the Communists. Nevertheless, despite an organized electoral fraud, the Communist Party did not manage to gain a majority on the so-called 'blue-ballot' elections held on 31 August 1947.

As an answer to the policy of containment, a new international organization called Cominform was established by the Soviet Union and its satellite states in the last days of September 1947. On the occasion of its first meeting, the participants learned that the age of tactical self-control was over, and in the short term the main goal in the region became that of Communist takeover. During the process of Stalinization (1947–9), the multiparty system was liquidated and a Communist unity party, called the Hungarian Working People's Party, was founded by the merger of the Hungarian Communist and Social Democratic parties. The omnipotent leader of the newly established totalitarian dictatorship was Mátyás Rákosi,[171] the procurator of Stalin. The last act of the takeover took place on 18 August 1949, when the parliament adopted a new Constitution modelled on the example of the 1936 Soviet Constitution, and Hungary was declared a 'People's Republic'.[172]

Terror became a part of everyday life. People declared as enemies of the regime were imprisoned or deported to labour camps. The strong arm of the political regime, the state police, called the State Protection Authority, organized show trials that often resulted in death sentences. Peasant estates were collectivized and their owners were forced to work on the new collective farms. As a consequence of Cold War tensions, the main economic goal became the forced development of heavy industry: as contemporary propaganda declared, Hungary was to become 'the land of iron and steel'. The unreasonable economic policy dictated by the Soviet Union resulted in chaos throughout the country.[173]

---

[171] Mátyás Rákosi was no relation of Jenő Rákosi.   [172] Gyarmati, *A Rákosi-korszak*, 112–65.
[173] Ibid., 166–219.

However, following Stalin's death on 5 March 1953, significant changes took place in Russian foreign policy. Rákosi was heavily criticized by the Soviet leadership, which 'invited' him to follow new directives and to share his power with somebody else. The Central Committee of the Hungarian Working People's Party faithfully followed Soviet instructions: Rákosi and his allies were excluded from the highest policymaking authority of the Party, the Politburo, and they exerted self-criticism. The new prime minister was Imre Nagy, during whose short tenure (4 July 1953 – 18 April 1955) a de-Stalinization of Hungarian politics began. To mention just two of his important measures, labour on the collective farms ceased to be obligatory and Gábor Péter, the head of the State Protection Authority, was sentenced to lifelong imprisonment.[174]

Due to the renewed tension in Russian–American relationships, this period of de-Stalinization did not last long. In October 1954, the US government invited the German Federal Republic to join the North Atlantic Treaty Organization; as a response, the countries of the Eastern Bloc, including Hungary, created the Warsaw Treaty Organization. In January 1955, Imre Nagy was heavily criticized for his radical reforms by Nikita Khrushchev and other members of the Soviet leadership in Moscow. Exploiting the new situation, Rákosi accused Nagy of 'right-wing deviation' and 'revisionism'. Nagy was discharged from his post and excluded from the Party. A process of re-Stalinization took place; forced collectivizations were resumed and the State Protection Authority became active again.[175]

However, Rákosi's regained power was short-lived. In 1955, tensions in the Soviet–American relationship began to relax: Soviet troops were withdrawn from Austria, and the leaders of the two great powers began negotiations on the occasion of the Geneva Summit. In February 1956, the politics of détente were sanctioned by the 20th Congress of the Communist Party of the Soviet Union, at which Khrushchev heavily criticized Stalin's personality cult and his offences against the law. By mid-July 1956, Rákosi, the man responsible for Stalinists' crimes in Hungary, had become so inconvenient that the Soviet leadership decided to discharge him from the post of First Secretary, and he consequently left the country.[176]

Although Rákosi's dismissal was welcomed by the opponents of Stalinism, his successor proved to be disappointing: Ernő Gerő was Rákosi's right-hand man and politically just as unacceptable. The situation became untenable, particularly after one of the victims of the show trials, the Communist László Rajk and his fellows, who had been executed in 1949 were legally

---

[174] Ibid., 328–57.   [175] Ibid., 358–75.   [176] Ibid., 376–93.

rehabilitated and reburied (6 October 1956). On 23 October, an anti-Soviet revolution broke out in Budapest following a mass demonstration at which some of the protesters had been shot dead. The leadership of the Communist Party tried to remedy the situation by dismissing Gerő and reappointing Imre Nagy as prime minister. During his short second tenure, Nagy reinstituted the multiparty system, formed a coalition government, initiated the withdrawal of Soviet troops, and declared Hungary's withdrawal from the Warsaw Pact. All of this happened with Soviet consent. At the end of October, however, the Soviet leadership changed its mind and on 4 November invaded Hungary. The Revolution was violently repressed, and the establishment of a new Soviet-installed government led by János Kádár meant the beginning of a new era in Communist Hungary.[177]

Theatrical Context: Operetta in Stalinist Hungary

In the summer of 1949, only one year after the revival of *La Belle Hélène*, radical changes were also taking place in theatrical life: the new political regime began to exert direct ideological control over theatrical institutions. According to the Ordinance of the Finance Minister dated 21 June 1949, all the capital's private theatres – even the Capital City Operetta Theatre – were nationalized.[178]

Another important change, not announced publicly, concerned the repertoire of the theatres: from the beginning of the 1949/50 season, theatre programmes were decided at meetings of the Ministry of Public Education, where the head of the portfolio himself presided.[179] Hence, during the tenure of József Révai, who led the Ministry between 1949 and 1953, all theatres became instruments of state propaganda, including the Capital City Operetta Theatre, whose programme between 1949 and 1956 fell into three main categories.[180] Of recent pieces by foreign authors, only those coming from the countries of the Soviet sphere of interest were programmed. In practice, this almost exclusively meant works by Soviet composers such as *Volny Veter* (Free Wind) by Isaak Iosifovich Dunayevsky,[181] *Trembita* by Yury Sergeyevich Milyutin,[182] and *Akulina* (based

---

[177] Ibid., 394–437.

[178] For the full text, see *A Vallás- és Közoktatásügyi Minisztérium színházi iratai* [Theatrical Documents of the Ministry of Religion and Public Education], vol. 2: *1946–1949*, ed. by Istvánné Dancs (Budapest: OSZMI, 1991), 194–207.

[179] For the control of theatres, see Gyöngyi Heltai, *Usages de l'opérette pendant la période socialiste en Hongrie, 1949–1956* (Budapest: Collection Atelier, 2011), 121–6.

[180] For the programme of the theatre, see Lajos Koch (ed.), *A Fővárosi Operettszínház műsora, 1923–1973* [The Programme of the Capital City Operetta Theatre, 1923–1973] (Budapest: Magyar Színházi Intézet, 1973), 58–63.

[181] Premiered as *Szabad szél* on 6 May 1950.   [182] Premiered as *Havasi kürt* on 18 May 1951.

on Pushkin's short story, *The Squire's Daughter*) by Iosif Naumovich Kovner.[183]

The most numerous layer of the repertoire was made up of new operettas by Hungarian authors. The plots of these works can be divided into two groups. The first group treated 'our progressive national traditions', that is, subjects taken from Hungarian history, reinterpreted according to the spirit of the Marxist theory of class struggle. A classic example of this type was *A szelistyei asszonyok* (The Women of Szelistye, premiered on 19 October 1951), based on Kálmán Mikszáth's novel of the same title (1901), set to music by István Sárközy. The other category portrayed on stage the utopian reality of the new political regime. Probably the most notorious example of this type was *Boci-boci tarka* (Cow, cow, colourful), whose highly intriguing subject was the collectivization of agriculture, and which ended with a folk-song suite in the style of Zoltán Kodály, accompanying the wedding of the tractor-driving bon vivant and the peasant prima donna. The production, which was set to music by Ottó Vincze, and in which two live calves also appeared on the stage, proved to be a real hit in the Eastern Bloc. Following the Budapest premiere, which took place on 3 July 1953, it was also performed in the German Democratic Republic as *Das buntscheckige Kälbchen*,[184] as well as in the Chinese People's Republic as *Hsiao Hua Niu Hsi Ko Chu*.[185] What is more, the company of the Operetta Theatre also performed it before the Soviet comrades, during its Moscow guest performance at the turn of 1955–6.[186]

The third category comprised Socialist Realist adaptations of old, classical operettas, primarily works by popular Austro-Hungarian authors but also including reworkings of two well-known pieces by Offenbach: *A gerolsteini nagyhercegnő* (*La Grande-Duchesse de Gérolstein*) (13 January 1950) and *Orfeusz* (*Orphée aux enfers*) (29 February 1952). As we shall see, however, the librettos of the old operettas were carefully expurgated of 'bourgeois decadence' and filled up with 'progressive' didactic content. Premiered on 12 November 1954, the new version of Emmerich Kálmán's *Die Csárdásfürstin*, rewritten by István Békeffi and Dezső Kellér, proved to be so popular that in effect it superseded the original piece on Hungarian stages.[187]

The latter production had already been premiered during the period of de-Stalinization, when changes of political direction apparently influenced the

---

[183] Premiered as *Az álruhás kisasszony* on 22 January 1954.

[184] German premiere: Rostock, Volkstheater, 24 February 1956.

[185] Chinese premiere: Peking, before 11 June 1957.

[186] See Gyöngyi Heltai, 'Operett-diplomácia: *A Csárdáskirálynő* a Szovjetunióban 1955–1956 fordulóján' [Operetta diplomacy: *Die Csárdásfürstin* in the Soviet Union at the turn of 1955–56], *Aetas* 19/3–4 (2004), 89 and 96–7.

[187] For a thorough analysis of the 1954 adaptation, see Heltai, *Usages de l'opérette*, 295–324.

programme policy of theatres. The détente also had important consequences in the practice of the state control of theatres. Following Imre Nagy's nomination as prime minister, József Révai was dismissed, and the new head of the Ministry of People's Education was the much more low-key István Dobi. Under his tenure, a kind of limited pluralism began in theatrical life, so much so that the Operetta Theatre acquired a rival: the Capital City Gaiety Theatre (Fővárosi Víg Színház), providing many more popular operetta productions – among others an adaptation of Offenbach's *Monsieur Choufleuri restera chez lui le ...* as *Egy marék boldogság* (A Handful of Happiness) on 29 April 1953. Nevertheless, the word 'limited' has to be emphasized: the rival institution was closed by the Ministry of People's Education in the summer of 1954, and its building became attached to the Operetta Theatre, serving as its second stage.[188] What is more, the same person held the role of director of the Operetta Theatre throughout the whole period between 1949 and 1956: Margit Gáspár. In this position she exerted such a significant influence over the Offenbach performances that her character and career are worth studying in detail.

Gáspár was born into a wealthy and cultivated bourgeois family in 1905.[189] Her uncle, Miksa Márkus, was a journalist; as the editor-in-chief of the daily newspaper *Magyar Nemzet* and member of the editorial board of another daily newspaper *Pesti Hírlap*, he had good relationships with the most influential politicians in the country. Under such circumstances, it is not surprising that Gáspár began her career in the interwar period as a journalist at *Pesti Hírlap* and *Új Idők*, two conservative newspapers. She also translated literary works from Italian, English, German, and French; it was she who published the first Hungarian version of Carlo Collodi's *The Adventures of Pinocchio* under the male pen name Miklós Gáspár.[190] Like Collodi's hero, she herself had a quite eventful and adventurous life. Her first husband was a Venetian chevalier named Mario Boni, but she also had a liaison with the Italian futurist poet Filippo Tommaso Marinetti. It was due to his influence that Gáspár became a member of Mussolini's Fascist Party during the 1930s. Although she did not mention it in the autobiographical novel she published in her later years,[191] she even delivered a paper on fascism at the Hungarian Academy of Sciences, under the title 'The New Italian Rinascimento', in which she claimed: 'Italy realized

---

[188] See Gyöngyi Heltai, 'A "nevelő szórakoztatás" válsága 1954-ben' [The crisis of 'educative entertaining' in 1954], *Korall* 14/51 (2013), 146–9.

[189] For her biography, see 'N. N.', 'Margit Gáspár', in *Új magyar életrajzi lexicon*, ed. Markó, vol. 2 (2001), 936.

[190] Carlo Collodi, *Pinocchio kalandjai: Egy kis fabáb története* [The adventures of Pinocchio: The story of a little wooden puppet], trans. by Miklós Gáspár, 3 vols. ([Budapest]: Nova, [1940–2]).

[191] Margit Gáspár, *Láthatatlan királyság: Egy szerelem története* [Invisible kingdom: The story of a love] (Budapest: Szépirodalmi Kiadó, 1985).

through Fascism that it had not only a past but also a future.'[192] In 1933, a photo appeared in the magazine *Színházi Élet* showing Gáspár performing the fascist salute along with Marinetti and several Hungarian actors.[193]

But how did Gáspár, Marinetti's beloved and a member of the Italian Fascist Party, became a Communist and director of the Operetta Theatre during the Rákosi era? Her experiences during World War II can help to explain this turn, which at first sight might seem to amount to an irresolvable contradiction. Because of her Jewish origins, the discriminatory laws also affected Gáspár's life. As attested by the official newspaper *Budapesti Közlöny*, in June 1941 she was deleted from the register of members of the Hungarian National Press Chamber.[194] As she confessed in her recollections, she and her mother managed to survive the terror of the Arrow Cross Party due to false documents;[195] her father had committed suicide earlier,[196] and she had assisted her terminally ill uncle in ending his life.[197] According to her memoirs, it was during the German occupation that she got in touch with members of the Communist movement, including Alajos Jámbor, who became deputy mayor of Budapest following World War II.[198]

The Márkus family played a significant role in the theatrical life of Budapest: Miksa and his two brothers, the architect Géza and the conductor Dezső, were the founders of the Folk Opera of the capital city, which opened in 1911. This can explain why Gáspár debuted as a stage author in 1933,[199] and why she became director of the Operetta Theatre in 1949. Until 1949, however, she had nothing to do with the genre of operetta. Following the end of World War II, she became the head of the press bureau of the Communist politician Zoltán Vas, and this acquaintance might also have contributed to her nomination. By then, Gáspár had manifested her abilities as director at the Municipal Theatre and the Hungarian Theatre where, on 9 June 1949, she first staged a Soviet operetta in Budapest. The piece in question was *Tabachny Kapitan* (Tobacco Captain)[200] by Vladimir Vladimirovich Shcherbachov and Nikolai Alfredovich Aduyev, and its music was arranged by Ferenc Farkas and Ottó Vincze.[201]

[192] 'N. N.', 'Margherita Boni előadása az új olasz rinascimentóról' [Margherita Boni's paper about the new Italian Rinascimento], *8 Órai Újság* 17/122 (2 June 1931), 9.
[193] *Színházi Élet* 23/20 (7–13 May), 19.
[194] N. N., 'Tagtörlések az Országos Magyar Sajtókamarában' [Deletion of members of the National Hungarian Press Chamber], *Budapesti Közlöny* 78/129 (10 June 1944), 2.
[195] Gáspár, *Láthatatlan királyság*, 475–8.   [196] Ibid., 422–3 and 430.   [197] Ibid., 437–9.
[198] Ibid., 472–3.
[199] Emil Balassa, '*Rendkívüli kiadás*: Gáspár Miklós vígjátéka a Belvárosi Színházban' [*Extra Edition*: Miklós Gáspár's comedy at the Inner City Theatre], *Magyar Hírlap* 43/28 (4 February 1933), 10.
[200] The title of the Hungarian production was *A dohányon vett kapitány* [The Captain Bought for Tobacco].
[201] *Vallomások a zenéről: Farkas Ferenc válogatott írásai* [Confessions about music: Ferenc Farkas's selected writings], ed. by László Gombos (Budapest: Püski Kiadó, 2004), 254.

Gáspár influenced the practice of operetta in Hungary not only as director of the Operetta Theatre but as a theorist and an author of pamphlets, as her short publication *Az operett* (The Operetta) attests.[202] As Gyöngyi Heltai has pointed out,[203] Gáspár formulated a myth of origin, according to which 'operetta is not a characteristic product of bourgeois society'; 'it was born not as the parody of opera during the "flourishing" of Capitalism', but instead should be understood as the successor of the *mimus*, a specific genre of ancient Roman popular theatre which was, according to her, 'a realist theatre in the genuine meaning of the word'.[204] Although she does not mention it here, from her later comments it is obvious that the realism she refers to ultimately points in the direction of Socialist Realism, which she regarded as 'realistic in the genuine meaning of the word'; she mentioned Soviet operettas as exemplary since 'they always mount collective problems on stage'.[205] According to Gáspár, ancient *mimus* 'always reflected reality in a playful and funny form, and the mirror held up to its own society was always at the same time a criticism of it'; what is more, '*mimus* always protected the suppressed against the suppressors', and 'it ridiculed the potentates of the earth with revolutionary boldness'.[206] She characterized the performers of the ancient *mimus* as examples of the 'people's democratic' operetta heroes, who

> unlike the actors of the tragedies, did not wear cothurnus: their naked soles threaded the earth. Most of them wore not even a mask: they showed their true face to the audience. . . . They played among the people, for the people, and were of the people; actors of proletarians, even themselves proletarian actors.[207]

Gáspár was clearly an expert in the forms of ancient eloquence, as the rhetorical devices used in the original Hungarian suggest: the polyptoton (among/for/of the people) and the chiasmus (actors of proletarians/proletarian actors). It should be noted, however, that she might have had only limited knowledge of ancient *mimus*. This form of Roman popular theatre became a literary genre relatively late (during the late Roman Republic) and only titles and shorter or longer fragments of *mimus* survive.[208] Accordingly, *mimus* could be used as the basis of a pleasing but shaky theory, whose main goal was the legitimation of the ideologically suspect operetta genre and the criticism of its pre-1945 traditions,

---

[202] Margit Gáspár, *Az operett* (Budapest: Népszava, 1949).

[203] Gyöngyi Heltai, 'Az operett eredetmítoszai és a politika: Egy "kitalált tradíció" a szocializmusban' [The myths of origin of operetta and politics: An 'invented tradition' during socialism], in Gyöngyi Heltai, *Az operett metamorfózisai, 1945–1956: A 'kapitalista giccs'-től a haladó 'mimusjáték'-ig* [The metamorphoses of operetta: From 'capitalist kitsch' to 'progressive mimus'] (Budapest: ELTE Eötvös Kiadó, 2012), 36–69.

[204] Gáspár, *Az operett*, 4.   [205] Ibid., 14.   [206] Ibid.   [207] Ibid., 4.

[208] About Roman mimus, see Gesine Manuwald, *Roman Republican Theatre* (Cambridge: Cambridge University Press, 2011), 78–83.

as well as the theoretical foundation of its Socialist Realist type. It is not incidental that *mimus* was the only genre of ancient Roman theatre in which female roles were played by women. Gáspár, however, did not mention that mime actresses showing 'their true face' performed not only with bare feet and without masks, but that they could appear naked or might be stripped nude during performances.[209] This practice can be explained by the fact that *mimus* performances were associated with the fecundity cult of Flora, the goddess of the flowering of plants, and they took place primarily (if not exclusively) during the festival known as Floralia.[210] This erotic aspect might have been central to the appeal of the genre, as an anecdote recorded by Valerius Maximus in his *Factorum ac dictorum memorabilium libri IX* suggests.[211]

Gáspár assumed a historical continuity between the practice of ancient *mimus* and Offenbach's operettas:

> The mimus . . . did not care about the anathema of the church, just as it did not fear the anger of Olympian deities earlier, in the pagan era. It represented them on the stage as satirically as its later offspring, Offenbach, did. More than 2000 years passed between the emergence of mimetic performances and the birth of Offenbach's works. Notwithstanding, if we analyse 'the operetta of antiquity' and the works created by the most ingenious mimus author of the modern age, we can recognize the same fundamental qualities in them. We can see that they are essentially identical. Likewise, if we see through the history of entertaining musical genres from the mimus theatre to Offenbach – through the burlesque popular farces of the Middle Ages and the richest flowering of extemporized play, the commedia dell'arte – we will recognize again the same characteristics in every period.[212]

According to Gáspár, these common characteristics were realism, satire, and optimism, and these create the long-lasting value of an operetta. By contrast, works lacking any of these characteristics 'are alien to the genre; they are inartistic and "kitschy", since everything that is reactionary is at the same time bad and perverts the genre'. According to her pseudo-historical argumentation, the heyday of the operetta was the nineteenth century, when it was an art of 'progressive spirit'. However, 'in capitalist society, which regards everything as "merchandise", it became a saleable ware, and the mass production of operettas began'. Under such circumstances, 'the operetta mocking the outgrowths of bourgeois society with a loose tongue (Offenbach!) did not meet the requirements of capitalism'. Hence, the new maecenas [i.e., bourgeois society]

---

[209] Ibid., 179.   [210] Ibid., 178.

[211] Book 2, chapter 10, section 8. For an English translation, see Valerius Maximus, *Memorable Doings and Sayings*, ed. and trans. by David Roy Shackleton Bailey (Cambridge, MA: Harvard University Press, 2000), vol. 1, 227–8.

[212] Gáspár, *Az operett*, 5.

'began to transform operetta into their own image and likeness'. Consequently, the genre 'began to lie'; 'from realistic art it became the most illusory kitsch'; and in this way 'the so-called operetta world emerged, in which on every Sunday a director-general is cooking in the pot of every typist girl'.[213] Quoting Stalin, she defined the task of transforming the genre as follows:

> The perverted operetta should be traced back to the route it travelled as an 'entertaining musical genre' over 2000 years. It should be reconducted to its natural maecenas, the people, in order to be able to once again 'take from the people's life and give to the people'.[214]

This was the theory of the Socialist Realist reform of operetta, which Gáspár first formulated in 1949 and subsequently developed into a book-length publication in 1963.[215] Her book appeared in German translation in 1969.[216] But how did this theory become practice?

Appropriating Offenbach

As already mentioned, the Capital City Operetta Theatre programmed two adaptations under Offenbach's name between 1949 and 1956. But what did the word 'adaptation' mean in these cases? As a response to this question, I quote here the synopsis of *A gerolsteini nagyhercegnő* as it was published in the theatrical programme-magazine *Színház és Mozi* at the time of the premiere:

> Act 1: In Gerolstein, the birthday of Grand Duchess Anna [Hanna Honthy][217] is celebrated by the court, and members of the government want to make her sign the 'Colibri Pact' and a contract concerning a transatlantic loan, called the Bratschild Plan. During a military parade, Grand Duchess Anna falls in love with Péter Milon [Pál Homm], an ordinary soldier from the province of Lundberg who had answered her questions with unusual sincerity. She promotes him. Péter's fiancée, Eszti, has walked on foot from Lundberg to Gerolstein in order to meet him. Overjoyed, the youngsters begin to dance at the watch post, but they are noticed by the commander-in-chief of the army, General Bumm [Kálmán Latabár]. Annoyed because Péter had expressed his opinion about the army food, he manacles the soldier. In her despair, Eszti has to appeal directly to the Grand Duchess, who orders him to be released. At her

---

[213] Ibid., 5–8. Gáspár is alluding here to a typical element of operetta plots: poor girls get rich lovers/husbands at the end of the piece.

[214] Ibid., 10.

[215] Margit Gáspár, *A múzsák neveletlen gyermeke* [The ill-bred child of the muses] (Budapest: Zeneműkiadó, 1963).

[216] Margit Gáspár, *Stiefkind der Musen: Operette von der Antike bis Offenbach*, trans. by Hans Skirecki (Berlin: Lied der Zeit, 1969).

[217] The names in square brackets – the actors performing the role in question – were added by the author.

command, the couple performs the dance objected to by Bumm before the court. Péter appeals to Anna so much that she eventually promotes him to general. According to the custom of Gerolstein, on the occasion of her birthday, the Grand Duchess gives the itinerant sword of the empire to a man of her choice. This time, Péter is chosen. Anna hands the sword to him and calls him to follow her into the palace.

Act 2: Péter Milon enters the palace with the set purpose of using his rank and power in the interest of Lundberg's people. His intention is supported by his countryman and friend, the head cook of the court, Jean Pudding [Tivadar Bilicsi]. The courtly faction does its best in order to win him over to its political aim, that is, [for Anna] to sign the pact and the loan contract, but to no avail. Péter and his friend are uncompromising. Péter is disappointed because the Grand Duchess does not call on him in order to repair the deranged affairs of the government. It is not in regard to politics that Anna has plans for her new general, but in regard to love. Seeing that all his efforts and good intentions are in vain, he suddenly resolves to leave the corrupt and vicious Grand Ducal court. Anna orders Péter's arrest and exile and then signs the pact and the loan contract. However, Péter and his friends cannot be captured because they have meanwhile arrived in Lundberg.

Act 3: One year has passed. Under Péter's leadership the province of Lundberg has revolted, seceded from Gerolstein, and declared its independence. The Gerolstein government issues an ultimatum to the province, in which it demands a return to the 'mother country'. The answer is a cold refusal. The people of Gerolstein are threatened by death from hunger, since Lundberg was their larder. Now, it is under such circumstances that the court is preparing for the celebration of the birthday of Grand Duchess Anna. The celebrations are interrupted by Bratschild's arrival [György Dénes]. The government cannot fulfil its contractual obligations, hence the palace will be sold by auction, confiscated things will be dragged away, and Gerolstein will be made into a golf course. The fate of the Grand Duchess's Empire has been decided.[218]

The synopsis faithfully summarizes the plot of the 'adaptation' – or rather the new piece –[219] which, according to the theatre playbill,[220] was made by the Working Team of the Capital City Operetta Theatre. However, as Gáspár confessed several decades later in an interview given to Sándor Venczel, the teamwork meant that the new text was written by the experienced operetta author, István Békeffi and the cabaret author Andor Kellér, while the main ideas were delivered by Gáspár

[218] N. N. '*A gerolsteini nagyhercegnő*', *Színház és Mozi* 3/2 (15 January 1950), 8.

[219] Two typewritten copies of the 1950 libretto are preserved in the Library of the Hungarian Theatre Museum and Institute, under the shelf marks Q 2349 and Q 19.419.

[220] A copy of the playbill of the premiere is kept in H-Bn, Playbills of the Capital City Operetta Theatre, 13 January 1950.

herself.[221] From Meilhac and Halévy's 1867 libretto[222] only the core character constellation remained: the Grand Duchess falls in love with an ordinary soldier, but he does not requite her love, since he has a fiancée. However, the miniature Cold War conflict and the political machinations affecting Gerolstein's fate are new, not to mention the denouement: the fall of the small state. As contemporary press reviews emphasized, these elements had an overt political message: they were intended to criticize the postwar economic recovery programme of the United States, the Marshall Plan, which was hostilely received in the Eastern Bloc. As the critic of *Szabad Nép*, the official daily newspaper of the Hungarian Working People's Party wrote,

> The theatre courageously transformed the old tale and rewrote the text so that the satirical edge targets the actual enemies of peoples. The Gerolstein which can be seen on the stage recalls some of the 'Benelux' or 'Fritalux' countries. It is today's suppressors and plunderers of small countries as well as the statesmen of the wangling, corrupt, stupid and cowardly lackey governments who appear on the stage. Who could not recognize in the 'bratschildized' Gerolstein the 'marshallized' countries, and who were not glad among the workers to see how the sellers of the homeland are overtaken by the fate of lackeys: the 'unselfish friend', the Western great power which provided them loan and pact, sells the whole country by auction.[223]

The characters also went through certain changes. In Melhac and Halévy's original, the Grand Duchess is memorable for her capriciousness and autocratic traits. What is more, she orders that the soldier (known as Fritz in the original) be assassinated, since her love remains unrequited. The motive of the planned assassination, however, was left out of the adaptation, which ended up being not particularly successful, despite the popularity of Hanna Honthy, who played the title role. The character called Jean Pudding is a completely new figure: his insertion can be explained in all likelihood by the popularity of the comic actor playing his part, Tivadar Bilicsi (1901–81).[224] But an even more significant difference is that the ordinary soldier, whose name is Péter Milon instead of Fritz, had been transformed into a freedom fighter who awakens to political self-awareness.

The 1952 adaptation of *Orphée aux enfers* was no less radical.[225] In this case, the new spoken texts were written by György Hámos (1910–76), who

---

[221] Sándor Venczel, 'Virágkor tövisekkel. Beszélgetés Gáspár Margittal' [A flourishing period with thorns: An interview with Margit Gáspár], *Színház* 32/8 (August 1999), 17.

[222] *La Grande-Duchesse de Gérolstein: Opéra-bouffe en trois actes, quatre tableaux par Henri Meilhac et Ludovic Halévy, musique de Jacques Offenbach* (Paris: Michel Lévy Frères, 1867).

[223] 'B. B.' [probably Béla Mátray Betegh], 'Egy operettsiker tanulságai' [Lessons of an operetta success], *Szabad Nép* 8/50 (28 February 1950), 6.

[224] For his biography, see Székely (ed.), *Magyar színházművészeti lexikon*, 94–5.

[225] A microfilm copy of the typewritten prompt book used at the Capital City Operetta Theatre is kept in H-Bn, Theatre Department, FM 6/6627 (Op. 132).

began his career in the 1930s as a journalist with *Pester Lloyd* and *Új Idők*. Following World War I, he worked in the Child Support Department of the Budapest Police Headquarters, but he also contributed to the postwar repertoire of the Capital City Operetta Theatre with the libretto of a Socialist Realist operetta entitled *Aranycsillag* (Golden Star, premiered on 3 November 1950 with Endre Székely's music) as well as the Hungarian translation of Dunayevsky's *Volny Veter.*[226] A libretto for the music numbers was provided by József Romhányi (1921–83),[227] a virtuoso poet and author of a volume of popular satirical animal fables entitled *Szamárfül* (Donkey's ear).[228] However, Gáspár might have contributed to this adaptation, too, since the new libretto shows significant similarities to one of her earlier spoken plays entitled *Új isten Thébában* (A New God in Thebes), a myth parody with a strong political message, which premiered at the Budapest Inner City Theatre on 7 June 1946.[229]

This time, the thrust of the piece targeted the alleged relationships between the Washington White House and the American underworld, so much so that Eurydice was carried down into the underworld by devils wearing Ku Klux Klan–like hoods. In contrast to the 1858 and 1874 librettos by Crémieux and Halévy,[230] in which Orphée is the director of the Thebes Conservatory and of rather easy virtue, the title hero was transformed into a 'peace-fighter' by Hámos, who was a member of the 'Countrywide Peace Council'. It should be noted that the main role was played alternately by the prose actor László Hadics and the operatic baritone László Palócz, who usually sang such roles as Iago in Verdi's *Otello* and Telramund in Wagner's *Lohengrin.*[231] In the new version, Eurydice (played alternately by two operetta prima donnas, Zsuzsa Petress and Marika Németh) is kidnapped by Pluto not for his own pleasure, but in order to put an end to the 'peace-mongering' of her husband. 'Peace-mongering' means that Orpheus has composed a Song of Peace whose performance tames wild animals and armed people.

---

[226] Later, from 1858, he was editor of the journal *Filmvilág* (Cinema world). For his biography, see Markó (ed.), *Új magyar életrajzi lexikon*, vol. 3 (2002), 90.

[227] For his biography, see Markó (ed.), *Új magyar életrajzi lexikon*, vol. 5 (2004), 796–7.

[228] József Romhányi, *Szamárfül* [Donkey's ear] (Budapest: Móra Ferenc Könyvkiadó, 1983).

[229] A typewritten script of the piece is kept at the Library of the Hungarian Theatre Museum and Institute, Q 12.307.

[230] *Orphée aux enfers : Opéra bouffon en deux actes et quatre tableaux par Hector Crémieux. Musique de Jacques Offenbach* (Paris: Michel Lévy frères, 1858). In 1874, this two-act version, which was premiered at the Théâtre des Bouffes-Parisiens in 1858, was transformed into a four-act spectacular *féerie*, whose first performance took place at the Théâtre de la Gaîté. The libretto of this latter version was published as *Édition conforme à la représentation au Théâtre de la Gaîté. Orphée aux enfers. Opéra-féerie en quatre actes, douze tableaux par Hector Crémieux. Musique de Jacques Offenbach* (Paris: Michel Lévy frères, 1874).

[231] For his biography, see Székely (ed.), *Magyar színházművészeti lexikon*, 588.

Hámos, the employee of the Child Support Department of the Budapest Police Headquarters, carefully banned adult content from the text, so much so that practically nothing remained of the frivolous marriage comedy on which it was based. In this version, Orpheus commits no adultery against his wife: on the contrary, they are a faithful couple who have just got married at the beginning of the piece. In contrast to Crémieux and Halévy's Orphée, who welcomes Eurydice's death with joyful relief, Hámos's hero, after having read Pluto's message, heroically decides to bring back his wife from the underworld – and, with her, of course, peace for mankind.

In Marxist terms, the Olympic deities play the role of the capitalist exploiter class: according to the new libretto, Mars drinks 'extra profit' while Jupiter is lobbying for war. The inhabitants of Olympus are willing to help Orpheus in bringing back his wife from the underworld, but only if the hero does not sing the Song of Peace, called a revolutionary song by Jupiter. The father of the gods calls Pluto on the phone and finds out that new sulphur mines have been detected, so the production of lightning can be increased. To put it another way, there will be enough arms to destroy the country of Prometheus, which is – translated into the language of myth – none other than an allegory of the Soviet Union.[232]

The denouement of *Orfeusz* is just as dramatic as that of *A gerolsteini nagyhercegnő*. According to the extant libretto, a trial takes place in Act 3, which is set in the underworld. Orpheus and Eurydice are accused by Jupiter and Pluto and are sentenced to remain in the underworld and to drink from Lethe, the river of forgetfulness. However, following the sentence, the Song of Peace can be heard off-stage, sung by the entire earth, and the despairing Mars brings disquieting news: in the Country of Prometheus, the lightning rod has been invented. Jupiter faints, and Cupid appears and declares the sentence of the people: Orpheus and Eurydice must be handed back. As can be seen, the closing scene is no less different from Offenbach's two versions than in the case of *A gerolsteini nagyhercegnő*. Nevertheless, it should be noted that at least the motive of the trial has an antecedent in Offenbach's 1874 *opéra-féerie* version. In that case, however, the accused is Pluto, the kidnapper of Eurydice, and the trial is rather light-hearted (one of the members of the tribunal, Minos, speaks in Auvergnat dialect, while another member, Eaque, has a Belgian accent).

One more figure is worth considering. Anti-clericalism is represented in the operetta by a new character, Jupiter's High Priest, whose predecessor could be presumed to have been Calchas from *La Belle Hélène*. However, the High Priest, who is addressed in the Catholic manner as 'Reverend Father',

---

[232] The same allegory also appears in Gáspár's play, *Új isten Thébában*.

believes he is receiving too few offerings. He condemns the desire for peace among the Greek people ('Do not stick your nose in Olympus's affairs! Deities know why war is necessary'). In a certain sense, he takes over the role of Crémieux and Halévy's Pluto: it is he who courts Eurydice in Orpheus's absence. Moreover, it should be noted that in the first cast, the High Priest was played by the same actor who played Pluto, György Dénes, which might have contributed to making the character even more negative. The anti-clerical message of the libretto was also heightened by the visual world of the performances, specifically by the costumes of the Olympic deities. Decades later, Gáspár tried to defend this element of the production as follows:

> I could not see the costume plans ahead of time; at that time, I was already not on friendly terms with Apáthi, the stage director (later we became good friends again); he could endure anywhere only for approximately one year, and in the second year he always quarrelled with the [company] director. Here, he carried out a kind of sabotage, so much so that the performance gained an anti-religious character, which was not my intention. On the occasion of the dress rehearsal, when I saw Jupiter in a white shirt with a halo around his head, I began to howl and I made him take it off. Certainly, it was also my fault because I did not check it in time.[233]

However, Róbert Rátonyi (1923–92), a popular comic actor and a member of the Operetta Theatre's troupe at that time,[234] who played the role of Mars in the production in question, recounted a different narrative of the affair. According to his recollections, Tivadar Bilicsi, the actor chosen for Jupiter's role, who was a religious man, expressed to Gáspár his antipathy towards the work, which was full of blasphemy in his opinion, and declined the role. The director tried to change his mind in vain. In the end, Jupiter was played by another actor, Gábor Agárdi (1922–2006), and Bilicsi left the company.[235]

It should be noted that at that time Offenbach's works were transformed into propaganda pieces not only at the Capital City Operetta Theatre but also elsewhere. This can be exemplified by the strongly reworked version of _M. Choufleuri restera chez lui le ..., Egy marék boldogság_, staged by the rival company of the Capital City Gaiety Theatre.[236] The spoken parts of the new libretto were written by István Fejér (1911–76), editor-in-chief of the programme-magazine _Színház és Mozi_ as well as the director of the Capital

[233] Venczel, 'Virágkor tövisekkel', _Színház_ 32/9 (September 1999), 39.

[234] For his biography, see Székely (ed.), _Magyar színházművészeti lexikon_, 642.

[235] Róbert Rátonyi, _Operett_ (Budapest: Zeneműkiadó, 1984), vol. 2, 290–2.

[236] The text of the adaptation is preserved as a typwritten script in H-Bn, Theatre Department, under the shelf mark MM 19.315.

City Gaiety Theatre,[237] while the author of the verse texts of the music numbers was a musicologist, Zsigmond László (1893–1981).[238] Their work was based not on the French original, attributed to a certain 'M. de Saint-Rémy',[239] who can be identified as Charles-August-Louis-Joseph de Morny, the stepbrother of Napoléon III, and Offenbach's protector.[240] As the names of characters attest (see Table 7), the authors instead used the Vienna adaptation, *Salon Pitzelberger*, by Carl Treumann, which was premiered there in October 1861. As Table 8 shows, this adaptation proved to be of decisive significance concerning the Hungarian performance history of the piece, even if translations of the French original also appeared on Hungarian stages. The Ofner Sommertheater had performed it as early as 1865, and its Hungarian translation was mounted on scene as late as 1985 in the capital.

The plot of *Monsieur Choufleuri restera chez lui le . . .* is set in a Paris salon and its first Paris performance took place likewise in a salon: that of the Presidential Palace of the Legislative Assembly. In *Salon Pitzelberger*, the salon was transposed to Vienna, while in the case of *Egy marék boldogság*, the setting is a country called 'Ladoméria'. Geographically, this place can be identified as Volodymyr of the one-time 'Königreich Galicien und Lodomerien', which from 1772 until 1918 belonged to the Habsburg Empire. However, since the end of World War I, it has been part of Ukraine; for the public of the 1953 Budapest performances, it might have seemed a faraway and almost imaginary setting.

The intrigues of *Monsieur Choufleuri* and that of *Salon Pitzelberger* are largely identical: a rich bourgeois wants to imitate the practice of contemporary aristocrats by organizing a musical soirée in his home. He invites three Italian singers who, however, do not arrive and the event is under threat of cancellation. In the end, it is the bourgeois gentleman, his daughter, and her lover who replace the singers, executing the so-called 'Trio italien', an amusing parody of the Italian operas of the 1830s. At the end, the father consents to the marriage of his daughter to her lover.

The name of the titular hero has different meanings in the different versions. Alluding to the non-aristocratic pedigree of the protagonist, Choufleuri derives from the French word 'chou-fleur', which means 'cauliflower'.[241] By contrast,

---

[237] For his biography, see Székely (ed.), *Magyar színházművészeti lexikon*, 208.

[238] For his biography, see Markó (ed.), *Új magyar életrajzi lexikon*, vol. 4 (2002), 118–19.

[239] *Comédies et proverbes par M. de Saint-Rémy* (Paris: Michel Lévy frères, 1865), 9–189.

[240] For Offenbach's relationship with Morny as well as Morny's collaboration with Hector Crémieux and Ludovic Halévy in writing the libretto, see Yon, *Jacques Offenbach*, 227 and 260.

[241] The name was taken over from a vaudeville by Dumanoir and Clairville and set to music by Florimond Hervé, one of Offenbach's contemporaries and another operetta composer. The piece in question was premiered at the Théâtre du Palais-Royal in 1953, and also published in print: *Les Folies dramatiques: Vaudeville en cinq actes par MM: Dumanoir et Clairville* (Paris: Michel Lévy frères, 1853).

Table 7 The names of characters in four versions of *Monsieur Choufleuri restera chez lui le* …

Role	*M. Choufleuri* (Paris, 1861)	*Salon Pitzelberger* (Vienna, 1861)	*Salon Jäschke* (Berlin, 1862)	*Egy marék boldogság* (Budapest, 1953)
The nouveau riche	Choufleuri	Pitzelberger	Jäschke	Kuffer
His daughter	Ernestine	Ernestine	Isolda	Katalin
Her lover	Babylas	Canafas	Arthur	Elemér
The groom	Peterman	Brösel	Peterman	Jóska
The soubrette	–	–	–	Piroska
The Italian singers	Sontag	Medori	Artôt	Medori
	Rubini	Bettini	Carrión	Bettini
	Tamburini	De Bassini	Formes	'Decassini'
The guests	M. and Mme Balandard	Herr and	M. and Mme	Brútusz
	M. and Mme Tilleuil	Frau von Krauthofer	Brettschneider	Baronne Stringl
		Herr and Frau von	Herr von Sonderlich	Father Poczek
		Schachtelhuber		Zsizsik Sr
		Herr von Stern		Zsizsik Jr
		Herr von Stutzl		
		Herr and Frau von Meyer		
		Herr von Stingelgruber		
		Fräulein Weinberlthee		
		Fräulein Schwab		

Table 8 The Budapest performance history of *Monsieur Choufleuri restera chez lui le ...*, 1863–2010

Premiere	Title	Theatre
18 Apr. 1863	*Choufleuri úr otthon lesz*	Folk Theatre
5 Feb. 1865	*Salon Pitzelberger*	Ofner Stadttheater
5 July 1871	*Choufleuri úr otthon lesz*	Endre Latabár's Troupe in the Buda Arena
13 May 1894	*Pitzelberger estélye*	City Park Arena
May 1899	*Piculás úr szalonja*	Dalos Theatre
15 Dec. 1912	*Káposztafi úr fogad*	Cabaret Ferenczy
1 Apr. 1921	*Az újgazdagok*	Capital City Orpheum
29 Apr. 1953	*Egy marék boldogság*	Capital City Gaiety Theatre
23 July 1985	*Pitzelberger úr szalonja*	Dominican Court of Hotel Hilton
14 Oct. 2010	*Italománia avagy operaest pezsgővel*	TV movie, Hungarian television

'Pitzelberger' is a derivative of the Austro-German verb 'pitzeln', whose meaning is 'to piddle about'.[242] The same figure is called 'Sebestyén Kuffer' in the 1953 Budapest version, and it should be noted that the word 'Kuffer' has a quite negative connotation in Hungarian. As a derivative of the German noun *Koffer*, its first meaning is 'suitcase' or 'luggage'; however, it can also mean 'woman's derrière', particularly if its size is quite considerable. With such a name, the protagonist is not only a farcical figure, but an expressively unsympathetic person. It should be noted that this character was played by the same Tivadar Bilicsi who had given up Jupiter's role in the case of the 1952 *Orfeusz*.

The role of Piroska, played by Ilona Serfőző (1926–88), is completely new. In the text attributed to Saint-Rémy, there is only a manservant without a female companion; Fejér's adaptation, however, in this respect follows the Austro-Hungarian tradition, where leading operetta roles usually included both a serious and a comic couple. It should be noted that even the figure of the manservant went through significant changes: the Belgian character Peterman, who impersonates an English groom, was transformed into an astute Hungarian servant called Jóska, played by the popular actor Gedeon Victor (1923–2004).

---

[242] For the explanation of the German word, I am grateful to Ralf-Olivier Schwarz.

There are significant differences concerning the names of the Italian singers, too. In Paris, the bourgeois gentleman wanted to invite the German soprano Henriette Sontag (1806–54), the Italian baritone Antonio Tamburini (1800–76), and the Italian tenor Giovanni Battista Rubini (1794–1854) to his soirée. These singers were quite reputed in the French capital in the 1830s, the time and place in which the plot of the operetta is set. Rubini and Tamburini were engaged at the Théâtre-Italien;[243] all three sang leading roles in works by Bellini and Donizetti, both in Italy and in Paris.[244] Although Sontag was not a member of the company of the Théâtre-Italien, she sang several times there from 1826, when she successfully debuted as Rosina in Rossini's *Il barbiere di Siviglia*.[245] In *Salon Pitzelberger*, Sontag, Rubini, and Tamburini were replaced by other contemporary singers active in Vienna: the Italian soprano Guiseppina Medori, the Italian tenor Geremia Bettini, and the Italian baritone Achille de Bassini. In the Berlin version,[246] the singers became the Belgian soprano Désirée Artôt, the Spanish tenor Emmanuel Carrión, and the German bass Karl Johann Formes. The 1953 Budapest libretto follows the Viennese version, except that De Bassini's name is misspelt as 'Decassini'.

Nevertheless, *Egy marék boldogság* shows even more important differences from *Monsieur Choufleuri* compared to *Salon Pitzelberger*. According to the Marxist theory of class struggle, the bourgeois and his guests are the enemies of the Communist regime. The range of enemies is quite wide: the guests of the Kuffer salon belong to very different social groups. The aristocracy is represented by a certain Baroness Stringl, the army by a military officer called Brúnó Brútusz, and the clergy by a priest named Father Poczek, while the bourgeoisie are represented by a rich landowner, Bertalan Zsizsik, and his son Zsozsó. They all belong to those groups of society which were stigmatized as 'reactionaries' in contemporary Communist phraseology. According to the new plot (which was inflated from one to three acts), Kuffer and his reactionary guests organize a conspiracy: they want to found an enterprise producing weapons. Some years after the devastation of World War II, at the time of the Cold War, this motive was sufficient to cause disgust in the audience. The motive of forced marriage is just as new as that of the conspiracy. Since the reactionaries need money in order

---

[243] *Almanach des spectacles de 1831 à 1834: Dixième année* (Paris: Barba, 1834), 28.

[244] See Péter Bozó, 'Offenbach and the Representation of the Salon', in *Musical Salon Culture in the Long Nineteenth Century*, ed. by Anja Bunzel and Natasha Loges (Woodbridge: The Boydell Press, 2019), 145.

[245] For her biography, see John Warrack, 'Henriette Sontag', in *The New Grove Dictionary of Music and Musicians*, www.oxfordmusiconline.com (accessed 19 May 2020).

[246] *Salon Jäschke: Operette in einem Aufzuge. Frei nach dem Französischen von E[mil] Pohl* (Berlin: Ed. Bote & G. Bock, 1862), www.digitale-sammlungen.de/?I=en (accessed 10 May 2020).

to realize their purpose, Kuffer wants to marry his daughter to Zsizsik's son. Needless to say, Katalin rejects the suggestion: firstly because the boy is a nitwit; secondly because she already has another lover, Elemér.

As might be suspected on the basis of this brief overview of the libretti, the music of the three above-mentioned works likewise went through significant changes – even if this factor of the production is by far not as well documented as the reworking of the plots. Unfortunately, no sound recordings, full scores, or orchestral parts survive. Nevertheless, from the contemporary press coverage of the productions, it is obvious that the music of *La Grande-Duchesse de Gérolstein* and *Orphée aux enfers* was arranged by Tibor Polgár (1907–93), a composer of popular music who later earned an international reputation as conductor of the Philharmonia Hungarica in West Germany (1962–4), that of the University of Toronto Symphony Orchestra (1965–6), and as a professor of the opera department at the University of Toronto (1966–75).[247] As four manuscript copies of the piano vocal score[248] of *A gerolsteini nagyhercegnő* used on the occasion of the Kecskemét premiere of the adaptation[249] might indicate, Polgár used Offenbach's music quite freely: he not only changed the original order of the music numbers but inflated the full score with several newly composed interpolations.

Even the music of *Egy marék boldogság* was thoroughly reworked, this time by László Várady (1906–89), a conductor who was active both at the Operetta Theatre (1949–57) and the Capital City Gaiety Theatre. Formerly a student of Zoltán Kodály and Leó Weiner at the Budapest Music Academy, he had had an international conducting career during the interwar period in such cities as Leipzig, Düsseldorf, Berlin, Bruxelles, Prague, and Paris.[250] Following World War II, he worked at the Szeged National Opera; then, after the Communist takeover, he became a key figure of Socialist Realist operetta in Budapest, not only as a conductor but sometimes also as a theorist.[251] After the 1956 revolution, he emigrated to Vienna, where he became a professor at the Hochschule für Musik and the Konservatorium der Stadt Wien, and founder of the Wiener Barockorchester.[252] According to the evidence of an extant handwritten vocal

[247] For his career, see Clifford Ford, 'Polgar, Tibor', in *The New Grove*, vol. 20, 30.

[248] H-Bn, Music Department, SZE 91. One of the copies bears the inventory number 1950/20.

[249] The Capital City Operetta Theatre's adaptation was premiered at the Kecskemét József Katona Theatre on 2 April 1950; that is, approximately three months after the Budapest premiere.

[250] It was he who conducted for the first time the first movement of Bartók's *Two Pictures* in the French capital in 1931. See Marcel Belvianes, 'Concerts-Poulet', *Le Ménestrel* 93/13 (24 March 1931), 142–3.

[251] See László Várady, 'A zene szerepe az operettben' [The role of music in operetta], *Új Zenei Szemle* 3/9 (September 1952), 8–11.

[252] For his biography, see Székely (ed.), *Magyar színházművészeti lexikon*, 840 and Markó (ed.), *Új magyar életrajzi lexikon*, vol. 6 (2007), 1060.

score of *Egy marék boldogság*,[253] Várady made use of several music numbers from such pieces as *La Fille du tambour-major*, *La Vie parisienne*, *Le 66*, *Les Deux aveugles*, the Barcarolle from *Les Contes d'Hoffmann* and the 'Galop infernal' from *Orphée aux enfers*. By contrast, from the original music of *Monsieur Choufleuri restera chez lui le* … , he retained only three pieces, among them the 'Trio italien' and the Trio No. 3, that is, exactly those numbers in which musical parody plays a significant role. Várady, however, treated the two numbers representing two different kinds of musical parody differently. While the music of the 'Trio italien' remained unchanged, the introduction to the Trio (No. 4), which included quotations from Boieldieu's *La Dame blanche* and Meyerbeer's *Robert-le-diable*, was cut.[254] His treatment is all the more understandable because the two operas quoted might have been unknown to contemporary audiences on the occasion of the 1953 production of *Egy marék boldogság*, since their local performances were limited to the period of the Habsburg Empire. The Budapest premiere of *Robert der Teufel* (a German version of *Robert-le-diable*) took place at the Pest Königlich-Städtisches Theater on 14 April 1834; the same work was also premiered in Hungarian, as *Ördög Róbert*, on 18 February 1843 at the Pest National Theatre.[255] The local premiere of *La Dame blanche* took place on 23 June 1864 at the Pest National Theatre.[256] After World War I, both pieces disappeared from the stage of the Budapest Opera House.

Offenbach as Political Property

'Let's let sexuality be the opium of the declining West!' – says Comrade Virág, a Communist character, in the popular Hungarian film, *The Witness* (*A tanú*, 1969), who finds the skirt of his secretary too short. Directed by Péter Bacsó, this movie, whose plot is an amusing satire of the early 1950s, proved to be so incisive that it was banned from release by Communist authorities. This sentence exemplifies the prudery and hypocritical attitude of the men in power, who – as we have seen – deprived even Offenbach's operettas of their erotic appeal.

---

253 H-Bn, Music Department, SZE 33.

254 For Offenbach and musical parody in general, see Siegfried Dörffeldt, 'Die musikalische Parodie bei Offenbach' (PhD diss., Johann-Wolfgang-Goethe-Universität, 1954). For a detailed analysis of the 'Trio Italien', see Bozó, 'Offenbach and the Representation of the Salon', 143–52.

255 For Meyerbeer's operas in Budapest, see Tibor Tallián, '"Opern dieses größten Meisters der Jetztzeit": Meyerbeer fogadtatása a korabeli magyar operaszínpadon' ["Opern dieses größten Meisters der Jetztzeit": Meyerbeer's reception on the contemporary Hungarian operatic stage], in *Zenetudományi dolgozatok 2004–2005* [Studies in musicology, 2004–2005], ed. by Sz. Farkas Márta (Budapest: MTA Zenetudományi Intézet, 2005), 1–60.

256 'A.' [probably Kornél Ábrányi], 'Nemzeti Színház' [National Theatre], *Zenészeti Lapok* (30 June 1864), 320.

Ironically, this was the same Péter Bacsó who in 1952 had published a review of *Orfeusz* in *Irodalmi Újság* after its premiere. His cautious criticism is typical of the atmosphere of the period and how political appropriation was perceived and received in the contemporary press.

As he wrote, 'it is a great merit of György Hámos that he recognized and further developed the impressively beautiful values of the original Orpheus myth'. On the other hand, he expressed his antipathy: 'the effect of the persiflage is weakened by the fact that the author often gratuitously over-politicizes his message; although satire can really achieve its goal by exposing types and connections, it cannot do so if the author unnecessarily makes his opinion of his characters clear at every turn through the use of journalistic devices taken from the daily press'.[257] Over-politicizing was, without doubt, a rightful criticism. It must be admitted, however, that even the reviewer used the politicized rhetorical clichés of the period, claiming that, 'in the wittiest way', Hámos had 'characterized the type of right-wing social democrat, who always refers to his crusted palms and his non-existing mass support right up until his lies are unmasked and he is clobbered by the working people who have been awakened to self-consciousness'.[258] At the same time, however, he correctly pointed out the primitivity of the work's 'positive symbolism', and even expressed 'what a primitive symbol of the Soviet Union is the country of Prometheus'.[259]

As is evident from Bacsó's review, even contemporary critics perceived the *Orfeusz* production as a politically charged propaganda performance. A similar opinion is expressed visually by an anonymous cartoon which was published, two months after the premiere of the adaptation, in the satirical magazine *Ludas Matyi* (see Figure 5).[260] In the caricature, entitled 'Orpheus in the Hell of Criticism', Offenbach himself can be seen addressing the following sentence to György Hámos, the author of the new libretto: 'Come, Gyuri, quickly, let us exert self-criticism.' Hámos's self-confident answer is as follows: 'Exert yourself, the text is good!' It should be noted that *Ludas Matyi* was not an impartial press organ: its jokes usually promoted Communist ideas. Self-criticism was a characteristic phenomenon of the Communist ritual: members of the Party who were found responsible for any mistake – particularly those who had lost their earlier power and influence – had to admit their crimes publicly. By inviting Hámos to self-criticism, the caricatured Offenbach encouraged readers to comply with the unwritten rules of the political regime. On the other hand, by rejecting self-criticism, Hámos is portrayed as an unrepentant dogmatist, chiefly

---

[257] Péter Bacsó, 'Orfeusz', *Irodalmi Újság* 3/6 (13 March 1952), 5. [258] Ibid. [259] Ibid.
[260] 'N. N.', 'Orpheusz a kritika poklában', *Ludas Matyi* 8/17 (24 April 1952), 39.

Figure 5 'Offenbach in the Hell of Criticism': caricature published in *Ludas Matyi* (24 April 1952)

responsible for the obvious failure of the piece, while Gáspár's and minister Révai's roles in the adaptation remain unmentioned.

At the season's closing meeting of the Capital City Operetta Theatre, even Gáspár herself admitted that the premiere of *Orfeusz* had proved to be unsuccessful. From her own words, as documented in the minutes, it also turns out that the team had tried to save the production through further reworking:

> The fact that today this theatre does not have a company but rather an ensemble was eloquently displayed when it was threatened with the danger of being disbanded. For example, after the unusual failure of the *Orfeusz* premiere, the company did not panic, did not act in haste, did not argue and did not try to shift the blame to each other, but instead collaborated. And after

working day and night for four days, we revamped *Orfeusz*, and it became as good as new.[261]

On the other hand, as the case of *A gerolsteini nagyhercegnő* examplifies, politically motivated adaptation did not provide a defence against the men in power, and a theatrical conception not in line with the actual expectations of Communist leadership could have inconvenient consequences. Characteristically, contemporary press reviews fail to mention this case, since publicity was controlled by the authorities. However, some private sources from the time and later recollections relate how the adaptation had had to be reworked because it was a little too close to reality.

Gáspár recalled the case in two interviews given several decades later, after the 1990 collapse of Communism. In the first interview, which appeared in the Socialist daily newspaper *Népszabadság*, she remembered how she had learned there were problems with the work:

> Approximately one week after the premiere, Miklós Molnár, leader of the cultural section of the journal *Szabad Nép*, appeared in the theatre and, following Act 1, he said that he was very sorry but this theatre is finished. There is no need for Honthys and Latabárs, no need for this countrified humour.[262]

It should be noted that Molnár did not express his negative opinion in the columns of *Szabad Nép*, despite the fact that it was he who edited the journal's cultural column. As Gáspár recalled in her 1993 interview, another acquaintance of hers, Rozália Vörös (Mrs Regényi), whose husband worked as department head at the Ministry of People's Education, had also warned her that the work had not been well received by the establishment, and she had suggested that Gáspár write to Mátyás Rákosi, the Secretary General of the Party himself. The director of the Operetta Theatre took Mrs Regényi's advice, and her letter addressed to Rákosi survives at the Hungarian National Archives. Since it so aptly reflects the atmosphere of the period, I quote it here in full:

Budapest,
18 January 1950

---

[261] H-Bn, Theatre Department, Fond 18/29: minutes of the season's closing meeting of the company of the Capital City Operetta Theatre held on 8 July 1952, page 2.

[262] Hanna Honthy (1893–1978) was the leading female star of the Operetta Theatre, despite her advanced age; Kálmán Latabár (1902–70) was an extraordinarily popular comic actor in the theatre. Árpád Pünkösti, 'A gerolsteini pártfőtitkár. Rákosi az operetthős, Feleki a vádlott' [The Party Secretary General of Gerolstein: Rákosi the operetta hero, and Feleki the accused], *Népszabadság* 51/173 (27 July 1993), 16.

To Comrade Mátyás Rákosi,

Secretary General of the Hungarian

Working People's Party

Budapest

As the director of the nationalized Capital City Operetta Theatre, I appeal to Comrade Rákosi to attend our new operetta, Offenbach's *The Grand Duchess of Gerolstein.*

To justify my request, I adduce the fact that the programming of this work caused a serious inner crisis in me and created severe contradictions for me, in the face of which I am puzzled. The matter is about whether the work I have done is a Communist work or a counter-revolutionary activity!

The nationalized Capital City Operetta Theatre premiered *The Grand Duchess of Gerolstein* on 13 January. Under my direction, the dramaturgical working team of the theatre completely reworked the text of the Offenbach work. Politically, the piece was a key work in its time, and now, we have transformed it into a pre-eminent modern-day political piece.

So, our Gerolstein became (despite the end-of-the-century costumes) a modern-day, Marshallized, Western small state, which is given over to American imperialism by its puppet government consisting of corrupt rascals and blockheads. Using the ancient devices of musical pamphlet, the work demonstrates how 'Gerolstein' will be plunged into poverty by the 'Bratschild loan', forced upon the state from overseas, as well as by the 'Colibry pact', and how 'Mr Bratschild', director general of the plan, will finally be expelled by the people. On the occasion of the premiere, the operetta met with success. The audience, which during the first three performances mainly consisted of seat holders who had come from the factories, laughed throughout the performance. Some cultural leaders who attended the performance found it very useful.

The first performance for a professional audience took place on Monday. Unfortunately, I got to know only the next day (in the intermissions I sojourned in the dressing rooms) that during act 2, a bigger group comprising several personalities of our theatrical life had gathered together. These people declared indignantly that the operetta [was] 'the counter-revolution itself', 'it [was] scandalous' and 'it [had to] be banned by all means'. Among other reasons for this, they gave the fact that when the hero, the ordinary soldier Péter Milon, is committed to trial, he exclaims the following: 'I do not defend myself, I accuse!' They understood this as if it were a quotation of Comrade Rákosi's words, which is inadmissible in an operetta. Needless to say, we did not have the intention of quoting

Comrade Rákosi. Nevertheless, due to this misapprehension, I began to wonder if the piece we had made with such good intentions was instead highly malignant.

If it can happen that the work I meant as a straightforward, humorous but educational, combative, party-spirited piece, is perceived by a certain group of theoretically well-trained comrades as counter-revolutionary, then there is something fatally wrong.

Either my eyes are bad, or theirs.

One thing is certain: if it is true that I am producing counter-revolutionary pieces in this post in which I have been placed, while believing that I have made a Communist work, then I cannot remain in my position, not even for a minute.

But this matter does not only decide my own fate. I reckon that the problem of the new operetta genre is a very important problem. And I also have to add that this indecorously gay, plain genre, which is a direct offspring of the old great public entertainment, the half-histrionic mime theatre, is handled with aristocratic petulance by one section of our cultural cadres. 'It is stupidity', they spit contemptuously, ashamed of having laughed at the jokes. 'This is not art', they declare, while failing to understand that the healthy entertainment of working people is a *physiological* problem, which passes beyond the frame of art.

Comrade Rákosi, maybe the theatre, whose leadership I was entrusted with by our Party, entertains poorly and harmfully. In this case, those responsible should be notified and the leader should be dismissed. But the need of working masses for laughter cannot be ignored! And it is useless if theoretically we are always declaring the importance of operetta yet when we see Latabár on the stage, this full-blooded comic actor of operetta, we wave him aside dismissively. Beyond my own problem, that is why I feel this strange and characteristic debate to be so important, one which became acute on the occasion of the first performance of *Grand Duchess of Gerolstein* for a professional audience. (And which has become ever more acute since then!) I consider it a great error that a section of our cultural cadres simply has no sense of humour. Hence, they break away from the playful masses, who long for optimistic laughter. They toe the line of those *precieuses* who think that 'high art' is necessarily identical to sleep-like boredom, and for whom everything which is well received by the masses is suspicious. In the past years, so many indecorously gay, unpretentious and radiantly joyful Soviet film operettas have come to us. Why do they not learn from them?! The workers of the Operetta Theatre think that they made a politically useful work (even if the piece and the performance is full of the faults and mistakes of a difficult beginning). If this work is harmful despite their efforts, this is only my fault. It is I who see something wrongly, and who led them in the wrong direction.

Comrade Rákosi, please, be my judge.

Liberty!

Margit Gáspár,

artistic director

of the Capital City Operetta Theatre[263]

The story does not end here. According to Gáspár's recollections, the 'next Saturday, instead of Rákosi, József Révai [the Minister of People's Education] appeared in the theatre' and attended the production in question.[264] Révai arrived accompanied by Antal Berczeller, Head of the Theatre Department of the Ministry, and after the popular comic actor Kálmán Latabár came on stage, 'he teared up with laughter'.[265] After having seen the performance, Berczeller wrote a lengthy report to Révai's secretariat on 27 January, in which he qualified the production in the following way: 'its political direction is good; its satire, unfortunately, does not reach Swift's or Cervantes's *niveau*, but rather represents that of the Pest cabaret'. He also quoted Péter Milon's incriminating passage mentioned in Gáspár's letter to Rákosi ('I do not defend myself, I accuse!'). However, he found that 'the sentence is appropriate here, and associating it with Comrade Rákosi's person and trial is leftist boastfulness, to say the least'.[266] Minister Révai himself, however, who on 31 January attached a supplement to Berczeller's report, had another opinion:

> To Comrade Rákosi!
> Fundamentally, I agree with Berczeller's report. I have also seen the performance, following Margit Gáspár's complaint. It is right that the operetta was updated and politicized. The performance is relatively good.
> The only fault of the text is that trial. On this point, Berczeller is wrong. This will be corrected by Margit Gáspár and her people. I. 31. Révai[267]

Now, what might have been the problem with 'that trial' in the operetta, whose 'political direction' was found to be otherwise 'good' by Berczeller? In my opinion, the contemporary audience might have perceived a similarity not so much to Rákosi's own two trials, but rather to the far-from paradisiac everyday

---

[263] National Archives of Hungary, MNL OL M-KS-276–65, Hungarian Working People's Party, Mátyás Rákosi's Papers as General Secretary, 1948–56.

[264] Pünkösti, 'A gerolsteini pártfőtitkár', 16.   [265] Ibid.

[266] National Archives of Hungary, MNL OL M-KS-276–65, Hungarian Working People's Party, Mátyás Rákosi's Papers as General Secretary, 1948–56.

[267] Ibid.

life of Stalinist Hungary, especially considering the fact that the premiere of the piece took place only months after the show trial of László Rajk and his companions. I think it highly likely that this is the reason why Révai found the trial scene in question problematic and found it necessary to correct it.

In the end, on 6 February, General Secretary Rákosi read Berczeller's report and Révai's commentary and wrote: 'Call Margit Gáspár. It is OK. Rákosi'. According to Rákosi's remark, it seems that following the phone call, the necessary changes were made to the operetta. This seems all the more likely because in 1950, Kálmán Latabár was awarded the Kossuth Prize by the Hungarian state 'for applying entertaining genres for the sake of progression, and particularly for his scenic representation in the operetta *A gerolsteini nagyhercegnő*'.[268] One year later, Gáspár was similarly honoured when she received the same Kossuth Prize 'for her successful work to initiate the formation of a new Hungarian operetta', according to the official announcement.[269]

After 1956, after Gáspár's resignation from her post of director of the Capital City Operetta Theatre, the direct propagandistic exploitation of Offenbach's pieces came to an end. Nevertheless, despite the Kádár regime's much more permissive cultural policy (1956–89), staging heavily altered adaptations instead of the composer's own pieces remained an established custom in Budapest. For example, the first post-revolution Offenbach premiere at the Operetta Theatre, *Szép Heléna* (*La Belle Hélène*), staged on 17 December 1959, was based on multiple adaptations. István Zágon's libretto, based on Egon Friedell and Hans Sassmann's 1931 Berlin version, had been reworked once again by Miklós Szinetár and Ferenc Karinthy and the music of this production also contained numbers composed by Tibor Polgár, as well as a rock-and-roll interpolation for the Spartan youngsters to perform. Under such circumstances, Imre Demeter, a critic of the production, accurately described the performance by remarking, 'Offenbach was not present.'[270] The influence of German-speaking theatrical practice also remained significant during the Kádár era, as is exemplified by the case of *Ritter Blaubart*. This adaptation of *Barbe-Bleue*, made by Walter Felsenstein and Horst Seeger and premiered at the Berlin Komische Oper on 24 September 1963, had a lasting impact in Hungary not only through its film version, released in 1973, but also through performance, when local

---

[268] 'N. N.', 'Az 1950. évi Kossuth-díjasok' [The Kossuth prize winners of the year 1950], *Szabad Nép* 8/63 (15 March 1950), 3.

[269] 'N. N.', 'Az 1951. évi Kossuth-díjasok' [The Kossuth prize winners of the year 1951], *Szabad Nép* 9/64 (16 March 1951), 2.

[270] Imre Demeter, '*Szép Heléna*', *Film, Színház, Muzsika* 3/52 (25 December 1959), 22–3.

audiences were able to see the East German company live on 11 May 1974.[271] What is more, at the beginning of the next decade, on 8 November 1981, the company of the Budapest Opera House mounted the work at the Erkel Theatre in István Iglódy's Hungarian translation with remarkable success.[272]

In one way or another, Offenbach had become a practically unknown composer by the arrival of the third millennium in Budapest. It seems, however, as if this situation has recently begun to change. In February 2015, *Orphée aux enfers* was revived at Müpa Budapest in a semi-staged performance and – it is important to emphasize – with the composer's own music.[273] Even the Hungarian premiere of his opera *Die Rheinnixen* by the company of the Opera House at the Erkel Theatre in February 2018 can be seen as a small but important step in this direction.[274]

* * *

In this study, I have sought to understand and explain the striking contrast between the Western European and Hungarian images of Offenbach around 2000, which are manifested in the unmistakable differences between the 2005 Budapest and 1998 Lyons productions of *Orphée aux enfers*, as well as in the lack of Hungarian-language secondary literature concerning the composer and his works. Thus, this brief survey of the period between 1920 and 1956 has sought to account for the factors which contributed to the different qualities and conventions of Offenbach performances in Budapest during this significant period in Hungarian history. As we have seen, local operetta traditions greatly affected the public image of the composer. In 1920 his figure and his works were used in a fictive tragic operetta following the popular Biedermeier type exemplified by *Das Dreimäderlhaus*. The antisemitism of the Horthy era subsequently had serious consequences for the composer's reputation: while in 1933, his *Les Brigands* was successfully staged at the Budapest Opera House, as a result of the implementation of the anti-Jewish laws, Offenbach's stage works were not allowed to be performed publicly between 1939 and 1944, and were staged only in closed performances by OMIKE Artist's Action. During the Stalinist period, the practice of staging pseudo-Offenbachian pieces continued,

---

[271] Károly Kristóf, 'A Komische Oper Offenbach-előadása: A Kékszakáll sikere' [The Offenbach performance of the Komische Oper: Success of *Bluebeard*], *Esti Hírlap* 20/110 (13 May 1974), [2].

[272] Péter Várnai, '*Kékszakáll*: Offenbach operettje az Erkel Színházban' [*Bluebeard*: Offenbach's Operetta at the Erkel Theatre], *Muzsika* 25/1 (January 1982), 19–21.

[273] Péter Bozó, 'VV Orfeusz feleséget keres' [VV Orpheus is looking for a wife], *Muzsika* 58/4 (April 2015), 29–31.

[274] Péter Bozó, 'Budapesti Offenbach-napok: A rajnai sellők, Kékszakáll' [Budapest Offenbach days: *Die Rheinnixen, Barbe-Bleue*], *Muzsika* 61/4 (April 2018), 18–23.

with politically charged propaganda adaptations at the Capital City Operetta Theatre and the Capital City Gaiety Theatre.

Since theatrical traditions do not change from one day to the next, it is not surprising that under the relatively unfavourable conditions in the mid-twentieth century, Offenbach performances in Budapest turned far away from their original texts and intents. In light of more recent productions, however, there is hope that more peaceful times will bring about a better understanding and more authentic performances of the works of this extraordinary composer, including in that city, where his works have enjoyed a long and fascinating legacy.

Bibliography

Primary Sources

Theatre Almanacs

Almanach des spectacles de 1831 à 1834: Dixième année (Paris: Barba, 1834)

Deutscher Bühnen-Almanach, vol. 24, ed. by Ludwig Schneider (Berlin: Hayn, 1860)

Deutscher Bühnen-Almanach, vol. 35, ed. by Albert Entsch (Berlin: n.p., 1871)

Librettos and Stage Manuals

Comédies et proverbes par M. de Saint-Rémy (Paris: Michel Lévy frères, 1865)

Édition conforme à la représentation au Théâtre de la Gaîté: Orphée aux enfers. Opéra-féerie en quatre actes, douze tableaux par Hector Crémieux. Musique de Jacques Offenbach (Paris: Michel Lévy frères, 1874)

Les Folies dramatiques: Vaudeville en cinq actes par MM: Dumanoir et Clairville (Paris: Michel Lévy frères, 1853)

H-Bn, Central Collection, 203.599: printed edition of song texts of *Die Banditen* in Richard Genée's German translation (Pest: Alois Bucsánszky, 1870)

H-Bn, Central Collection, 820.502: printed libretto of *Hoffmann meséi*, translated by Antal Várady, Jakab Béla Fái, and Antal Radó (Budapest: Károly Müller, 1900)

H-Bn, Music Department, ZBK 201/h: manuscript copies of some roles without music used in the 1933 premiere of *A banditák* at the Royal Hungarian Opera House

H-Bn, Theatre Department, FM 6/6627 (Op. 132): a microfilm copy of the typewritten prompt book of *Orfeusz* used at the Capital City Operetta Theatre

H-Bn, Theatre Department, IM 1146: a printed libretto of *Offenbach* by Jenő Faragó and Mihály Nádor, German translation by Robert Bodanzky and Bruno Hardt-Warden (Vienna: Eirich, [1922])

H-Bn, Theatre Department, MM 333: libretto of *Chopin* by Jenő Faragó and István Bertha (Budapest: Sándor Marton, 1927), lithographed from the manuscript prompt book of the Király Theatre

H-Bn, Theatre Department, MM 5292: a manuscript prompt book and stage manual of *Casanova* by Jenő Faragó and Izsó Barna, used at the Budapest Folk Theatre

H-Bn, Theatre Department, MM 6935: a manuscript stage manual of *A rablók* from Ignác Krecsányi's estate. István Toldy's translation

H-Bn, Theatre Department, MM 13.884: a manuscript prompt book of *A rablók* from Ignác Krecsányi's estate. Endre Latabár's translation

H-Bn, Theatre Department, MM 16.286: prompt book of *Szép Heléna* used at the Budapest Scala Theatre in 1920; Frigyes Karinthy's autograph manuscript

H-Bn, Theatre Department, MM 16.562: a printed libretto of *Offenbach* by Jenő Faragó and Mihály Nádor (Budapest: Sándor Marton, 1921)

H-Bn, Theatre Department, MM 18.750: a printed copy of *Eljegyzés lámpafénynél*, Hungarian translation by Miklós Feleki (Pest: Herz János, 1860)

H-Bn, Theatre Department, MM 19.315: a typewritten script of *Egy marék boldogság*

H-Bn, Theatre Department, Víg. 370: a manuscript copy of *Három a kislány* used as a stage manual for the Gaiety Theatre performances; Zsolt Harsányi's translation

La Grande-Duchesse de Gérolstein: Opéra-bouffe en trois actes, quatre tableaux par Henri Meilhac et Ludovic Halévy, musique de Jacques Offenbach (Paris: Michel Lévy Frères, 1867)

Library of the Hungarian Theatre Museum and Institute, Q 2349: a typewritten libretto of the 1950 adaptation of *A gerolsteini nagyhercegnő*

Library of the Hungarian Theatre Museum and Institute, Q 12.307: a typewritten script of *Új isten Thébában* by Margit Gáspár

Library of the Hungarian Theatre Museum and Institute, Q 19.419: a typewritten libretto of the 1950 adaptation of *A gerolsteini nagyhercegnő*

Music Collection of the Hungarian Radio, 15-41/B: stage manual of *Offenbach* by Jenő Faragó and Mihály Nádor (Budapest: Sándor Marton, 1921), lithographed from the manuscript stage manual of the Király Theatre

Orphée aux enfers: Opéra bouffon en deux actes et quatre tableaux par Hector Crémieux. Musique de Jacques Offenbach (Paris: Michel Lévy frères, 1858)

Salon Jäschke: Operette in einem Aufzuge. Frei nach dem Französischen von E[mil] Pohl (Berlin: Ed. Bote & G. Bock, 1862)

Music Scores

H-Bn, Music Department, Ms. mus. 10.930/1–3: Mihály Nádor's autograph full score of *Offenbach*

H-Bn, Music Department, Népsz. 694/III–V: orchestral parts used in the 1920 reprise of *Szép Heléna*

H-Bn, Music Department, SZE 33: a handwritten copy of the piano vocal score of *Egy marék boldogság*

H-Bn, Music Department, SZE 91: four manuscript copies of the piano vocal score of *A gerolsteini nagyhercegnő*

Hungarian State Opera House, without shelf mark: a printed vocal score of *Eljegyzés lámpafénynél* with handwritten entries, including the 1860 cast list of the National Theatre production

Statistical Yearbooks

Budapest székesfőváros statisztikai közleményei, vol. 15/2: *Budapest fővárosa az 1881. évben* [Statistical publications of the capital city Budapest, vol. 15/2: The capital city Budapest in 1881], ed. by József Kőrösi (Budapest: Ráth Mór, 1882)

Budapest székesfőváros statisztikai közleményei, vol. 33/2: *Budapest fővárosa az 1901-ik évben. A népszámlálás és népleírás eredményei* [Statistical publications of the capital city Budapest, vol. 33/2: The capital city Budapest in 1901. Results of the census], ed. by József Kőrösy and Gusztáv Thirring (Budapest: Grill Károly, 1905)

Budapest székesfőváros statisztikai közleményei, vol. 52: *Az 1920. évi népszámlálás előzetes eredményei* [Statistical Publications of the Capital City Budapest, vol. 52: Preliminary Results of the 1920 Census], ed. by Gusztáv Thirring (Budapest: Budapest Székesfőváros Statisztikai Hivatala, 1921)

Archival Sources

H-Bn, Theatre Department, Fond 4/96: Records of the Pest National Theatre

H-Bn, Theatre Department, Fond 18/29: minutes of the season's closing meeting of the company of the Capital City Operetta Theatre held on 8 July 1952

H-Bn, Theatre Department, Irattár 152, fol. 3: typewritten circular to the members of the OMIKE Artist's Action

National Archives of Hungary, Hungarian Working People's Party, Mátyás Rákosi's Papers as General Secretary, 1948–56

Theatre Playbills and Programme Booklets

H-Bn, Theatre Department, playbills of the Pest National Theatre

H-Bn, Theatre Department, OMIKE. Programme booklets of the OMIKE Artist's Action

Periodicals

8 Órai Újság
A Hon
A Zene
Az Ojság
Budapesti Hírlap
Budapesti Közlöny
Esti Hírlap
Film, Színház, Muzsika
Fővárosi Lapok
Haladás
Irodalmi Újság
La France musicale
Le Ménestrel
Ludas Matyi
Magyar Hírlap
Magyar Zsidók Lapja
Magyarság
Muzsika
Napkelet
Népszava
Neue Freie Presse
Pester Lloyd
Pesth-Ofner Localblatt und Landbote
Pesti Hírlap
Pesti Napló
Prager Tagblatt
Szabad Nép
Színház és Divat
Színház és Mozi
Színházi Élet
Színházi Látcső
Új Nemzedék
Új Zenei Szemle
Világ
Vossische Zeitung
Zenei Hét
Zenei Szemle

Zeneközlöny
Zenelap
Zenészeti Lapok

Other Testimonies

Dancs, Istvánné. *A Vallás- és Közoktatásügyi Minisztérium színházi iratai* [Theatrical documents of the Ministry of Religion and Public Education], 2 vols. (Budapest: OSZMI, 1991)

Fényes, Elek. *Magyarország geographiai szótára, mellyben minden város, falu és puszta, betürendben, körülményesen leiratik* [Geographical dictionary of Hungary, in which every city, village, and wilderness is circumstantially described in alphabetical order], vol. 3 (Pest: Kozma Vazul, 1851)

Gáspár, Margit. *Az operett* [The operetta] (Budapest: Népszava, 1949)

Gáspár, Margit. *A múzsák neveletlen gyermeke* [The ill-bred child of the muses] (Budapest: Zeneműkiadó, 1963)

Gáspár, Margit. *Stiefkind der Musen: Operette von der Antike bis Offenbach*, trans. by Hans Skirecki (Berlin: Lied der Zeit, 1969).

Gáspár, Margit. *Láthatatlan királyság: Egy szerelem története* [Invisible kingdom: The story of a love] (Budapest: Szépirodalmi Kiadó, 1985)

Gombos, László (ed.). *Vallomások a zenéről: Farkas Ferenc válogatott írásai* [Confessions about music: Ferenc Farkas's selected writings] (Budapest: Püski Kiadó, 2004)

Komor, Ágnes. *Apám, Komor Vilmos* [My father, Vilmos Komor] (Budapest: Táltos GM, 1986)

Offenbach, Jacques. "'Concours pour une opérette en un acte'", *La France Musicale* 3/148 (17 July 17, 1856), 6–7.

Offenbach, Jacques. *Offenbach en Amérique: Note d'un musicien en voyage, précédée d'une notice biographique par Albert Wolff* (Paris: Calmann Lévy, 1877)

Offenbach, Jacques. *Egy muzsikus útinaplója: Offenbach Amerikában*, trans. by Mária Peterdi, introduction by Sándor Fischer (Budapest, Zeneműkiadó, 1960)

Pünkösti, Árpád. 'A gerolsteini pártfőtitkár: Rákosi az operetthős, Feleki a vádlott' [The Party Secretary General of Gerolstein: Rákosi the operetta hero, and Feleki the accused]. *Népszabadság* 51/173 (27 July 1993), 16

Rátonyi, Róbert. *Operett*, 2 vols. (Budapest: Zeneműkiadó, 1984)

Schumann, Robert. *Gesammelte Schriften über Musik und Musiker*, 4 vols. (Leipzig: Wigand, 1854)

Schumann, Robert. *On Music and Musicians*, ed. by Konrad Wolff, trans. by Paul Rosenfeld (Berkeley: University of California Press, 1983)

Venczel, Sándor. 'Virágkor tövisekkel. Beszélgetés Gáspár Margittal'. *Színház* 32/8 (August 1999), 16–21; 32/9 (September 1999), 39–42; 32/10 (October 1999), 46–8

Valerius Maximus. *Memorable Doings and Sayings*, ed. and trans. by David Roy Shackleton Bailey (Cambridge, MA: Harvard University Press, 2000)

Secondary Literature

Books

Baranello, Micaela. *The Operetta Empire: Music Theatre in Early Twentieth-Century Vienna* (Oakland: University of California Press, 2021)

Batta, András. *Träume sind Schäume: Die Operette in der Donaumonarchie*, trans. by Maria Eisenreich (Budapest: Corvina Kiadó, 1992)

Binal, Wolfgang. *Deutschsprachiges Theater in Budapest* (Vienna: Böhlaus Nachfolger, 1972)

Bozó, Péter. *Fejezetek Jacques Offenbach budapesti fogadtatásának történetéből* [Chapters from the history of Jacques Offenbach's Hungarian reception] (Budapest: Rózsavölgyi és Társa Kiadó, 2021)

Braham, Randolph L. *A népirtás politikája: A holocaust Magyarországon* [*The politics of genocide: The Holocaust in Hungary*] trans. by Tamás Zala (Budapest: Belvárosi Könyvkiadó, 1997)

Braham, Randolph L. *The Politics of Genocide: The Holocaust in Hungary* (New York: Columbia University Press, 3/2016 [1/1981])

Csáky, Moritz. *Ideologie der Operette und Wiener Moderne: Ein kulturhistorischer Essay zur österreichischen Identität* (Vienna: Böhlau, 1996)

Dahlhaus, Carl. *Nineteenth-Century Music*, trans. by J. Bradford Robinson (Berkeley: University of California Press, 1989).

Dörffeldt, Siegfried. *Die musikalische Parodie bei Offenbach* (PhD diss., Frankfurt am Main: Johann-Wolfgang-Goethe-Universität, 1954)

Everist, Mark. *The Empire at the Opéra: Theatre, Power and Music in Second Empire Paris*. Cambridge Elements in Musical Theatre (Cambridge: Cambridge University Press, 2021)

Everist, Mark. *Opera in Paris from the Empire to the Commune* (New York: Routledge, 2019)

György Gyarmati. *A Rákosi-korszak* [The Rákosi era] (Budapest: ÁBTL–Rubicon, 2013)

Gyurgyák, János. *A zsidókérdés Magyarországon* [The 'Jewish question' in Hungary] (Budapest: Osiris Kiadó, 2001)

Gyurgyák, János. *Ezzé lett magyar hazátok: A magyar nemzeteszme és nacionalizmus története* [Your Hungarian homeland became like this: A history of Hungarian nationalism] (Budapest: Osiris Kiadó, 2007)

Gyurgyák, János. *Magyar fajvédők* [Hungarian race-protectionists] (Budapest: Osiris Kiadó, 2012)

Harsányi, László. *A fényből a sötétbe: Az Országos Magyar Izraelita Közművelődési Egyesület, 1909–1950* [From light into darkness: The National Hungarian Jewish Cultural Association, 1909–1950] (Budapest: Napvilág Kiadó, 2019)

Heltai, Gyöngyi. *Usages de l'opérette pendant la période socialiste en Hongrie, 1949–1956* (Budapest: Collection Atelier, 2011)

Heltai, Gyöngyi. *Az operett metamormfózisai, 1945–1956: A 'kapitalista giccs'-től a haladó 'mimusjáték'-ig* [The metamorphoses of operetta: From 'capitalist kitsch' to 'progressive mimus'] (Budapest: ELTE Eötvös Kiadó, 2012)

Horák, Magda. *Ősi hittel, becsülettel a hazáért! Országos Magyar Izraelita Közművelődési Egyesület, 1909–1944* [With ancient faith and honour for the homeland! The National Hungarian Jewish Cultural Association, 1909–1914] (Budapest: Háttér, 1998)

Karady, Victor and Péter Tibor Nagy (eds.). *The Numerus Clausus in Hungary: Studies on the First Anti-Jewish Law and Academic Anti-Semitism in Modern Central Europe* (Budapest: Pasts Inc. Centre for Historical Research, History Department of the Central European University, 2012)

Manuwald, Gesine. *Roman Republican Theatre* (Cambridge: Cambridge University Press, 2011)

N. Mandl, Erika. *Színház a magyar sajtóban a két világháború között* [Theatre in the Hungarian press in the interwar period] (Budapest: Argumentum Kiadó, 2012)

Poriss, Hilary. *Changing the Score: Arias, Prima Donnas, and the Authority of Performance* (Oxford: Oxford University Press, 2009)

Prokopovych, Markian. *In the Public Eye: The Budapest Opera House, the Audience and the Press, 1884–1918* (Vienna: Böhlau Verlag, 2014)

Romsics, Ignác. *A Horthy-korszak* [The Horthy era] (Budapest: Helikon Kiadó, 2017)

Romsics, Ignác. *Hungary in the Twentieth Century* (Budapest: Corvina Kiadó, 2/2010)

Romsics, Ignác. *Magyarország története a XX. században* [Hungary in the twentieth century] 3rd edition (Budapest: Osiris Kiadó, 2003)

Schwarz, Ralf-Olivier. *Jacques Offenbach: Ein Europäisches Portrait* (Weimar: Böhlau Verlag, 2019)

Schwarz, Ralf-Olivier. *Vaudeville und Operette: Jacques Offenbach's Werke für das Théâtre du Palais-Royal* (Fernwald: Burkhard Muth, 2007)

Senelick, Lawrence. *Jacques Offenbach and the Making of Modern Culture* (Cambridge: Cambridge University Press, 2017)

Sipos, Balázs. *Sajtó és hatalom a Horthy-korszakban* [Press and power in the Horthy era] (Budapest: Argumentum Kiadó, 2011)

Tallián, Tibor. *Magyar képek: Fejezetek a magyar zeneélet és zeneszerzés történetéből, 1940–1956* [Hungarian pictures: Chapters of the history of Hungarian musical life and composition, 1940–1956] (Budapest: Balassi/ MTA BTK, 2014)

Traubner, Richard. *Operetta: A Theatrical History*, 2nd edition (New York: Routledge, 2003 [1st edition 1980])

Walton, Benjamin. *Rossini in Restoration Paris: The Sound of Modern Life* (Cambridge: Cambridge University Press, 2007)

Yon, Jean-Claude. *Jacques Offenbach*, 2nd edition (Paris: Gallimard, 2010 [1st edition 2000])

Edited Volumes

Dohr, Thomas, Kerstin Rüllke and Thomas Schipperges (eds.). *Bibliotheca Offenbachiana* (Cologne: Verlag Dohr, 1998), Beiträge zur Offenbach-Forschung, ed. Christoph Dohr, vol. 1.

Franke, Rainer (ed.). *Offenbach und die Schauplätze seines Musiktheaters* (Laaber: Laaber-Verlag, 1999)

Gajdó, Tamás (ed.). *Magyar színháztörténet* [Hungarian theatre history], vol. 2: *1873–1920* (Budapest: Magyar Könyvklub/OSZMI, 2001)

Gajdó, Tamás (ed.). *Magyar színháztörténet* [Hungarian theatre history], vol. 3: *1920–1949* (Budapest: Magyar Könyvklub, 2005)

Kerényi, Ferenc (ed.). *Magyar színháztörténet* [Hungarian Theatre History], vol. 1: *1790–1873* (Budapest: Magyar Színházi Intézet, 1990)

Lévai, Jenő (ed.), *Írók, színészek, énekesek és zenészek regényes életútja a Goldmark-teremig. Az OMIKE színháza és művészei* [A novelistic biography of writers, actors, singers and musicians to the Goldmark Room. The theatre and artists of the National Hungarian Jewish Cultural Association] (Budapest: Faragó, 1943)

Lévai, Jenő (ed.). *The Writers, Artists, Singers, and Musicians of the National Hungarian Jewish Cultural Association (OMIKE), 1939–1944*, expanded edition by Frederick Bondy, trans. by Anna Etawo (West Lafayette, IN: Purdue University Press, 2017)

Mathew, Nicholas and Benjamin Walton (eds.). *The Invention of Beethoven and Rossini: Historiography, Analysis, Criticism* (Cambridge: Cambridge University Press, 2013)

Schmierer, Elisabeth (ed.). *Jacques Offenbach und seine Zeit* (Laaber: Laaber-Verlag, 2009)

Staud, Géza (ed.). *A budapesti Operaház 100 éve* [100 years of the Budapest Opera House] (Budapest: Zeneműkiadó, 1984)

Essays in Edited Volumes

Ackermann, Peter. 'Eine Kapitulation: zum Verhältnis Offenbach–Wagner', in *Jacques Offenbach: Komponist und Weltbürger*, ed. by Winfried Kirsch und Ronny Dietrich (Mainz: Schott's Söhne, 1985), 135–48

Bozó, Péter. 'Offenbach and the Representation of the Salon', in *Musical Salon Culture in the Long Nineteenth Century*, ed. by Anja Bunzel and Natasha Loges (Woodbridge: The Boydell Press, 2019), 139–52

Brzoska, Matthias. 'Jacques Offenbach und die Operngattungen seiner Zeit', in *Jacques Offenbach und seine Zeit*, ed. by Elisabeth Schmierer (Laaber: Laaber-Verlag, 2009), 27–36

Everist, Mark. 'Jacques Offenbach: The Music of the Past and the Image of the Present', in Mark Everist and Annegret Fauser (eds.), *Music, Theater, and Cultural Transfer: Paris, 1830–1914* (Chicago: The University of Chicago Press, 2009), 72–98

Everist, Mark. 'Mozart and *L'impresario*', in Michelle Biget-Mainfroy and Rainer Schmusch (eds.), *L'esprit français und die Musik Europas. Entstehung, Einfluss und Grenzen einer ästhetischen Doktrin. Festschrift für Herbert Schneider* (Hildesheim: Georg Olms, 2007), 420–33

Hooker, Lynn M. 'Hungarians and Hungarianisms in Operetta', in Anastasia Belina and Derek B. Scott (eds.), *The Cambridge Companion to Operetta* (Cambridge: Cambridge University Press, 2020), 61–75

Péteri, Lóránt. 'Idyllic Masks of Death: References to *Orphée aux Enfers* in "Das himmlische Leben"', in Jeremy Barham (ed.), *Rethinking Mahler* (New York: Oxford University Press, 2017), 127–37

Tallián, Tibor. '"Opern dieses größten Meisters der Jetztzeit": Meyerbeer fogadtatása a korabeli magyar operaszínpadon' ['Opern dieses größten Meisters der Jetztzeit': Meyerbeer's reception on the contemporary Hungarian operatic stage], in *Zenetudományi dolgozatok 2004–2005* [Studies in musicology, 2004–2005], ed. by Sz. Farkas Márta (Budapest: MTA Zenetudományi Intézet, 2005), 1–60

Journal Articles

Heltai, Gyöngyi. 'Operett-diplomácia: A Csárdáskirálynő a Szovjetunióban 1955–1956 fordulóján' [Operetta diplomacy: Die Csárdásfürstin in the Soviet Union at the turn of 1955–56], Aetas 19/3–4 (2004), 87–118.

Heltai, Gyöngyi. 'A két háború közti pesti operett stiláris és ideológiai dilemmái: A Király Színház példája (1920–1936)' [Stylistic and ideological dilemmas of the interwar Budapest operetta: Through the example of the Király Theatre (1920–1936)], Tánctudományi Közlemények 3/1 (2011), 53–68 (part 1); 3/2 (2011), 33–75 (part 2)

Heltai, Gyöngyi. 'A 'nevelő szórakoztatás' válsága 1954-ben' [The crisis of 'educative entertaining' in 1954], Korall 14/51 (2013), 146–9

Mácsai, János. 'Az OMIKE zenei előadásai, 1939–1944' [The musical performances of OMIKE, 1939–1944], Magyar Zene 52/4 (November 2014), 441–51

Mondelli, Peter. 'Offenbach's Bouffonnerie, Wagner's Rêverie: The Materiality and Politics of the Ineffable in Second Empire Paris', Opera Quarterly 32/2–3 (2016), 134–59

Tallián, Tibor. 'Az OMIKE Művészakció operaszínpada, 1940–1944' [The operatic stage of the OMIKE Artist's Action, 1940–1944], Muzsika 39/1 (January 1996), 14–18

Tallián, Tibor. 'Népoperai kezdeményezések a századelő Budapestjén' [Popular operatic enterprises in turn-of-the-century Budapest], Muzsika 40/10 (October, 1997), 13–16

Willson, Flora. 'Future History: Wagner, Offenbach, and "la musique de l'avenir" in Paris, 1860', Opera Quarterly 30/4 (2014), 287–314

Yon, Jean-Claude. 'La création du Théâtre des Bouffes-Parisiens (1855–1862) ou la difficile naissance de l'opérette', Revue d'Histoire moderne et contemporaine 39 (October–December, 1992), 575–600

Yon, Jean-Claude. 'La carrière posthume d'un musicien ou Offenbach aux enfers', Histoire, économie et société 22/2 (2003), 261–73. (This article is a reworking of the epilogue of a book-length monograph)

Encyclopaedias

Ehrmann-Herfort, Sabine. 'Operette', in Handwörterbuch der musikalischen Terminologie, ed. by Albrecht Riethmüller, vol. 4 (Stuttgart: Steiner, 1972), 1–20

Kutsch, K. J. and Leo Riemens (eds.). Großes Sängerlexikon, 7 vols. (Munich: Saur, 2003)

Markó, László (ed.). Új magyar életrajzi lexikon [New Hungarian biographical lexicon], 6 vols. (Budapest: Magyar Könyvklub/Helikon Kiadó, 2001–7)

Schöpflin, Aladár (ed.). *Magyar színművészeti lexikon* [Hungarian lexicon of theatre arts], 4 vols. (Budapest: Országos Színészegyesület és Nyugdíjintézete, 1929–31)

Sadie, Stanley (ed.). *The New Grove Dictionary of Music and Musicians* (Oxford: Oxford University Press, 2001), www.oxfordmusiconline.com

Székely, György (ed.). *Magyar színházművészeti lexikon* [Hungarian lexicon for theatre arts] (Budapest: Akadémiai Kiadó, 1994)

Catalogues and Repertoire Lists

Koch, Lajos. *A Fővárosi Operettszínház műsora, 1923–1973* [The programme of the Capital City Operetta Theatre, 1923–1973] (Budapest: Magyar Színházi Intézet, 1973)

Loewenberg, Alfred. *Annals of Opera – 1597–1940* (London: John Calder, 1978)

Molnár, Klára. *A Népopera – Városi Színház, 1911–1951* [The folk opera – Municipal Theatre, 1911–1951] (Budapest: OSZMI, 1998)

Acknowledgements

For financial support of my research, I am indebted to the Hungarian Scientific Research Fund (OTKA) as well as to the Board of Trustees of the János Bolyai Research Scholarship of the Hungarian Academy of Sciences. For their help, I would like to express my warmest thanks and gratitude to the complete staff of the Music Department as well as the Theatre Department of the Széchényi National Library, Budapest (in particular to Ildikó Sirató, Magdolna Both, Katalin Szende, and Enikő Korláth). My special thanks go to Gyöngyi Heltai for the very inspiring conversations with her. I also have to thank the following persons and institutions: Mirella Csiszár (Library of the Hungarian Theatre Museum and Institute/Országos Színháztörténeti Intézet és Múzeum Könyvtára); Mihály Sárdi (Budapest Operetta Theatre/Budapesti Operettszínház); Györgyi Nagy, Hajnalka Németh, and Veronika Menyhárt (Archive and Music Collection of the former Hungarian Radio/Magyar Rádió Archívuma és Kottatára); Márton Karczag (Music Collection of the Hungarian State Opera House/Magyar Állami Operaház Kottatára), Klára Somogyi and Adrien Csabai (Research Library of Music History of the Liszt Academy of Music/Liszt Ferenc Zeneművészeti Egyetem Zenetörténeti Kutatókönyvtára); Katalin Jankovich-Bésán (Library of the former University of Theatre and Film Arts/Színház- és Filmművészeti Egyetem Könyvtára); as well as Mária Benyovszky (Library of the Institute for Musicology/Zenetudományi Intézet Könyvtára). For the thorough revision of my English text, I am indebted to Shane MacMahon, Brian McLean (†), and the editor of the *Elements in Musical Theatre* series, my distinguished colleague William Everett.

Cambridge Elements ☰

Elements in Musical Theatre

William A. Everett

University of Missouri-Kansas City

William A. Everett, PhD is Curators' Distinguished Professor of Musicology at the University of Missouri-Kansas City Conservatory, where he teaches courses ranging from medieval music to contemporary musical theatre. His publications include monographs on operetta composers Sigmund Romberg and Rudolf Friml and a history of the Kansas City Philharmonic Orchestra. He is contributing co-editor of the *Cambridge Companion to the Musical* and the *Palgrave Handbook of Musical Theatre Producers*. Current research topics include race, ethnicity and the musical and London musical theatre during the 1890s.

About the Series

Elements in Musical Theatre focus on either some sort of 'journey' and its resulting dialogue, or on theoretical issues. Since many musicals follow a quest model (a character goes in search of something), the idea of a journey aligns closely to a core narrative in musical theatre. Journeys can be, for example, geographic (across bodies of water or land masses), temporal (setting musicals in a different time period than the time of its creation), generic (from one genre to another), or personal (characters in search of some sort of fulfilment). Theoretical issues may include topics relevant to the emerging scholarship on musical theatre from a global perspective and can address social, cultural, analytical, and aesthetic perspectives.

Cambridge Elements ⹀

Elements in Musical Theatre

Elements in the Series

Printed in the United States
by Baker & Taylor Publisher Services